# LET'S GET CRACKING!

## The How-To Book of Bullwhip Skills

Second Edition

By Robert Dante

With Sylvia Rosat

Copyright 2016 by Robert Dante

All rights reserved. No part of this book may be used or reproduced in any manner whatsoever without the written permission of the Publisher.
Printed in the United States

Library of Congress cataloging-in-Publication Data
Dante, Robert 1953-

Let's Get Cracking! The How-To Book of Bullwhip Skills
by Robert Dante

ISBN
EAN-13

# CONTENTS

Photo Credits . . . . . . . . 5

Preface to Second Edition . . . . . . . 7

Forward to First Edition by Andrew Conway . . . . . . . 8

A Note on Translations . . . . . . . 9

**Chapter 1 – Whips** . . . . . . . 13
First Things First – Learning the Lingo – A Whip's Anatomy –
The Physics Behind It All – The Real Source of the Whip's Crack –
Different Types of Whips – Wild West Whips

**Chapter 2 – A Foundation for Good Whip Cracking** . . . . 21
Getting a Good Grip – Belly Up – Creating Safety Zones –
Point and Squeeze – Practicing with Both Hands

**Chapter 3 – The Basic Cracks** . . . . 29
The Circus Crack – The Overhand Flick – The Cattleman's Crack –
The Flip Back

**Chapter 4 – The Right Whip** . . . . 37
What to Look For – Plaits and Braids – Long Whip vs Short Whip –
Wrist Loops – The Key to Getting a Good Whip – Caring for Your Whip –
Sure, Your New Whip is Stiff

**Chapter 5 – Improve Style** . . . . 47
Setting the Whip – Pulling the Trigger – Foot Position – Getting the Most
Out of Practice – Listening to Your Whip – Twelve Principles of Whip Artistry

**Chapter 6 – Poppers** . . . . 55
Making Your Own Poppers – The Double Twist Method – The Chopstick
Method - Knotting Your Popper – Variations - Attaching Your Popper –
Dante's Favorite Attachment Knot

## Contents – continued

**Chapter 7 – Single Whip Routines & Flashes** . . . . 63
Slow Figure 8s - Fast Figure 8s - Cow & Calf -
Snake Killer - Flourishes - Pausing the Crack - Coachman's Crack -
Volleys - Arrowhead - Plane Variations

**Chapter 8 – Two-Handed Whip Cracking** . . . . 76
Two-handed Timing Terms – The Train – Windshield Wipers –
Florentines – Queensland Crossovers – Parting Shots

**Chapter 9 – Tricks and Stunts** . . . . 80
Safety – Styrofoam Strips – Popping Balloons – Playing Cards –
Snuffing Candles – Slicing Bananas – Newspaper – Wraps &
Grabs – Poker Chip Off Tongue – Flying Streamer Cut

**Chapter 10 – Performing** . . . . **97**
Be Professional – Create a Character – Choreography – Rehearsing –
Using Black Lights – Dress the Part (Costumes) – Assistants – Venues –
Handling Tangled Lashes – Dancing on the Edge

**Chapter 11 – Teaching Others** . . . . 108
Safety First – Teaching Tips

**Chapter 12 – In the Whip Zone** . . . . 112

### Appendices

1. Two Practice Routines    116
2. Safety Protocols    119
3. Can Kids Crack Whips?    120
4. Frequently Asked Questions    122
5. Getting Ready for Spring    126
6. Sample Show Scripts    127
7. Your Whip Repair Kit    133
8. Free Flyers    134
9. The Perfect Whip Throw    140
10. Whips as Exercise    141
11. One Dozen Ways to    142
    Improve Accuracy

# PHOTO CREDITS

Page 1 -

Page 2

Page 3

Page 4

Page 5

6 || Let's Get Cracking!

## PREFACE TO THE SECOND EDITION

"Do the thing, and you have the power," said R.W. Emerson. He was right.

Whip cracking is no longer a fringe activity practiced only by Wild West desperadoes, superheroes or urban subterranean creatures of the night. These days there are many good whip makers, fine bullwhip artists and top-notch teachers available wherever you are, thanks to the internet.

I am pleased to thank bullwhip artist and whipmaker Sylvia Rosat for her invaluable contributions to the foreign-language versions of this book, and for her willingness to share photos of the bullwhip experience with readers around the world.

This book differs from the first edition more in form than in content. New material has been added;. have clarified the text by calling the whip's cracker or lash a "popper," since the word "cracker" Is also used to describe the whip handler.

This edition has new pictures and an appendix of pages you can photo copy for your own use. Please understand I am not telling you how YOU should do any of the tricks or stunts in this book. I am only telling you how I do it. Make each trick your own. In short, don't perform MY tricks – perform YOUR tricks. Make this your own journey. As Andrew Conway says, "Think of it as a pilgrimage. The important thing is not being there, it's going there."

I refer to the assistant, the Target Girl, as "She." No sexism is intended. Female whip crackers use Target Boys, and people of the same gender can assist each other in whip acts, as well. Oh, the poverty of the English language...!

If there are any errors the blame falls solely on my shoulders. I will try to do better next time.

-Robert Dante-
2016

## FORWARD TO FIRST EDITION

In Silverton Oregon lies Cyrus W. Barger_(1847-1924), buried at his request with a whip in his hand, just as he used to hold it when he drove a stagecoach. A whip was such an important symbol of a stagecoach driver that they were called whips, just as the guard on the back was called the shotgun. It seems that old Cyrus Barger wasn't sure where he was going, but wherever it was, he thought a whip might come in handy.

There is something about a good whip that makes you not want to let go, in Cyrus's case even after he had let go of life itself. A whip has its own life, its own spirit, its own energy. Like a fine sports car or a racing yacht, a good whip can be both a work of art and a perfect machine. If you read this book carefully, you will see that it is about more than just the mechanics of cracking a whip. It is about the spirit of the whip itself.

Does this sound too philosophical? Well, never mind, the way of the whip is a pragmatic one, too, with tangles or welts to punish misjudgment, and a perfect crisp clear crack when you find the true path. And what better guide could you have on this path than Robert Dante?

If you watch Robert cracking a whip you will see the same grace and economy of motion as a Tai Chi_master. The whip and the wielder move as a single organism, in sensuous curves punctuated by vibrant cracks. Such apparent ease is the product of years of dedicated practice and study. In this book, Robert shares what he has learned in those years. Of course, you still have quite a bit of practice ahead of you before you are as good as he is, but it will be easier for you than it was for him as you have his experience to help you.

Welcome, everyone, to the magic of Robert Dante.

Andrew Conway
2008

# A NOTE ON TRANSLATIONS

## By Sylvia Rosat

French and German do not have equivalents of some English words and expressions related to whip cracking. Even just the expression "whip cracking" in itself doesn't exist. In French, you would say you crack whips ( which in French sounds really weird), but for the name whipcracking there is no translation.

Happily, Sylvia Rosat created a table of French whipcracking vocabulary, which is here reproduced.

The terms are translated when possible, or kept in English with French definitions of what they mean, in order to make learning easier and to keep everyone on the same page.

*English: Whipcracker*
Français: Whipcracker ou pratiquant du fouet artistique
Définition: Personne qui pratique le whipcracking

*English: Whip*
Français: Fouet
Définition: Un fouet est un instrument tressé de plusieurs lanières de cuir , nylon , dacron ou autre materiel.

*English: The crack*
Français: Le crack
Définition: L' orsque l' on claque un fouet , le bruit qu' il produit s' appele le crack qui n est autre qu 'un mini bang supersonique. Quand un fouet produit un crack son extremité ( le cracker) à alors passé la vitesse du son.

*English : The cracker*
Français : Le cracker
Définition: Le cracker est la partie du fouet qui va produire le crack ( le son du fouet ) , en franchissant la barrière du son. Du au stress causé par le crack sur le cracker, celui -ci va s'user au bout d' un moment et devra etre changé assez fréquemment.

*English : The loop*
Français : La boucle
Définition : Courbe qui se forme naturellement dans le corps( thong) du fouet lorsqu' on le fait claquer. Cette boucle doit avoir lieu pour que le fouet claque.

*English: Basic cracks*
Français : Les cracks de bases ou mouvements de bases
Définition :Les cracks de bases regroupent un ensemble de mouvements de bases dans la technique du whipcracking. Il existe également plusieurs variations de ces cracks de bases. Dans les compétitions australiennes, chaque crack de base correspond à un certain nombre de points variant selon la difficulté du mouvement.Les participant exécutent un enchainements de mouvements ou tous les cracks doivent etre clairs et entendus par les juges.

*English : Rythmic routine*
Français : Routine rythmique
Définition : Enchainement de cracks de bases et de leurs variations avec un ou deux fouets créant des rythmes avec les crack émis.

*English: Single handed routine*
Français : Routine en simple commande
Définition: Routine , enchainement avec un fouet

*English : Double handed routine*
Français : Routine en double commande
Définition : Routine , enchainement avec deux fouets

*English : Targeting*
Français : Le targeting, faire du targeting

Définition: Une des différentes disciplines du fouet artistique est le targeting. Cette discipline
demande beaucoup de précision .Cela consite à couper , bouger, attraper,... un objet ( fleurs , foulards, cigarette, journal ,etc..) avec le fouet tout en produisant un crack.

*English : The target*
Français: La cible
Définition: L' objet ou les objets que vous allez utiliser pour le targeting.

*English: Wraps,body wraps*
Français: Enroulés, faire des enroulés , wraps
Définition: Une autre discipline du fouet artistique sont les wraps . Cela consiste à enrouler lefouet autour d¢ un objet ou d' un assistant tout en produisant le crack ,.... et bien sûr sans blesser votre assistant!

*English: Stand*
Français: Support
Définition: Support utilisé pour fixer les cibles pour le targeting.

*English: Fire whip*
Français: Fouet enflammé, fouet en feu
Définition:Fouet en kevlar spécialemment conçu pour l¢ utilisation de performances feu.

*English: Whipmaker*
Français: Artisan tresseur de fouets
Définition: Personne qui fabrique les fouets.

## 12 || Let's Get Cracking!

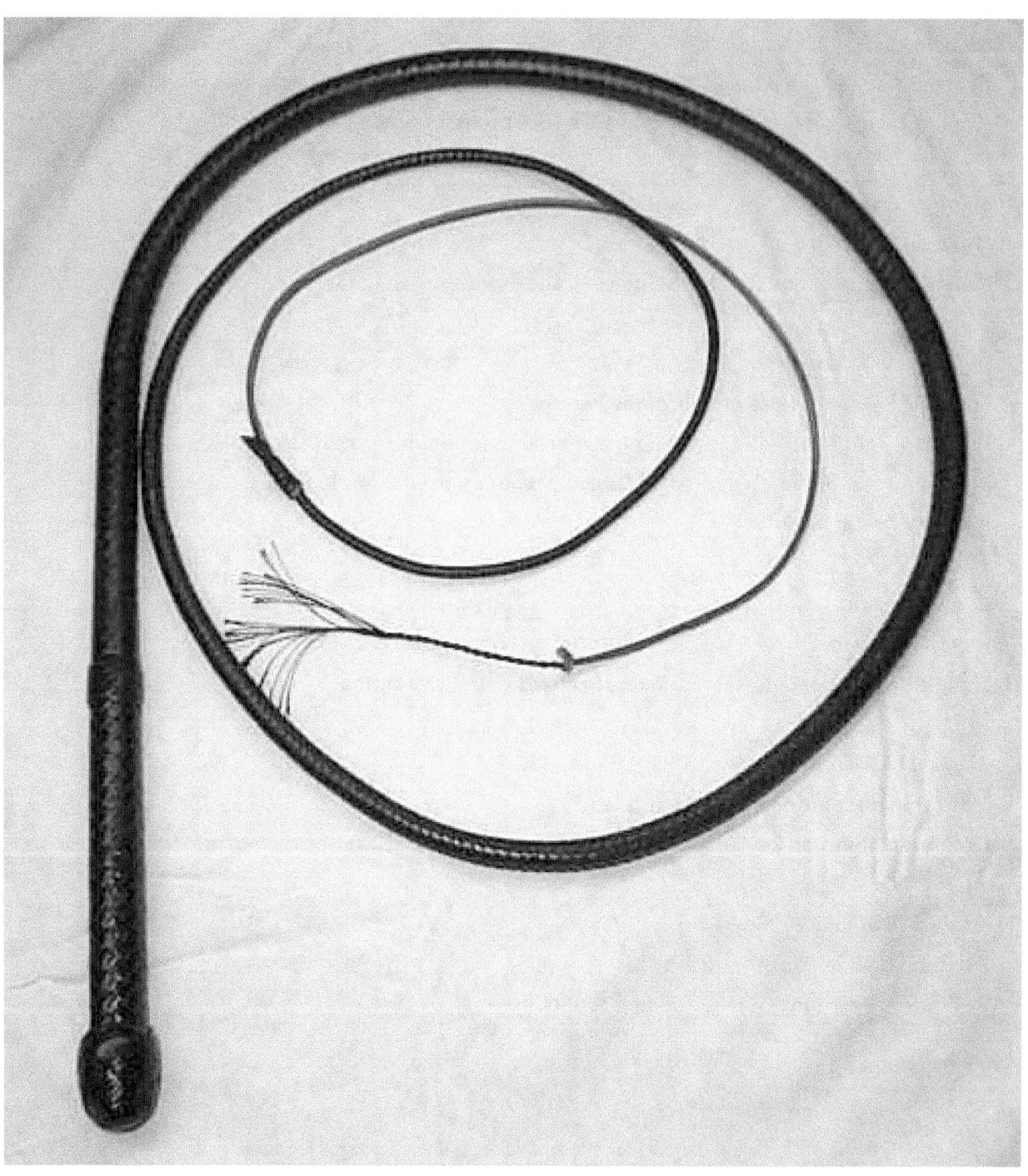

# Chapter 1 – Whips

**First Things First** – **Learning the Lingo** – **A Whip's Anatomy** – **The Physics Behind It All** – **The Real Source of the Whip's Crack** – **Different Types of Whips** – **Wild West Whips**

## First Things First

1. Protect your eyes! Wear safety goggles or glasses, especially when you are learning something new.

2. Wear a hat with a wide brim, like a cowboy hat or a fedora. This will catch the whip when it comes back to slash your face, and it will protect your ears (a baseball hat won't). Even with a wide-brimmed hat and safety glasses, you may still catch one across the face, so if you are sensitive about your looks, don't be ashamed to put on a helmet with a visor. A motorcycle helmet or fencer's mask can give you that full protection, but it might get a bit heavy on the head after a while.

3. If your ears are sensitive, wear ear plugs or sound suppressing headphones like the ones worn by shooters.

4. Wear long pants and sleeves. Even plain cotton can mitigate a painful whack. A shirt will not stop you from being hit, but it may soften the impact. Leather, of course, will protect you well.

Beginners are frequently nervous around a whip, which is not a bad thing. The danger is that after they've been cracking for a while, they may become overconfident and jump headfirst into trying new moves and harder combinations before they're ready. Most of the accidents I have seen are due to whip crackers letting their focus wander. That's when the whip punishes them for not paying attention.

### Learning the Lingo

Just as beginners can become bewildered by the lack of common terms for identical cracks and whips, they may also be baffled when they encounter the same word being used to describe different things. Take a deep breath and accept that you will always be wrong in someone else's eyes. This should not stop you. You're in good company.

For example, a whip's fall can be either an Australian style (a long, sinuous, rounded 'shoelace' attached to the thong) or a Texas style (a flat 'slapper' which is an extension of the thong itself). They are both falls.

The end of the handle is called the Turk's Head (when it is a braided ball covering the end of the handle). It can also be called the butt of the whip, or the knob, or the knot.

At the other end of the whip, that tasseled string tied to the fall is called the popper. In some circles, it is called the cracker. Some people call it the lash. In bygone days, they called it the snapper. They are all correct.

Starting to get the idea? Sometimes, it's like trying to find a seat at the Mad Hatter's tea party. Don't worry about it. Develop a healthy sense of humor. I guarantee that you will hear experienced whip crackers occasionally josh each other on this issue ("Say, was that a flick or an overhand throw?" "Yep!").

### A Whip's Anatomy

This is the definition of a whip: A single-tail whip is a flexible, tapered thong in which one end is thrown out to form a moving loop, and the other end is attached to a momentarily stationary point like a hand or handle.

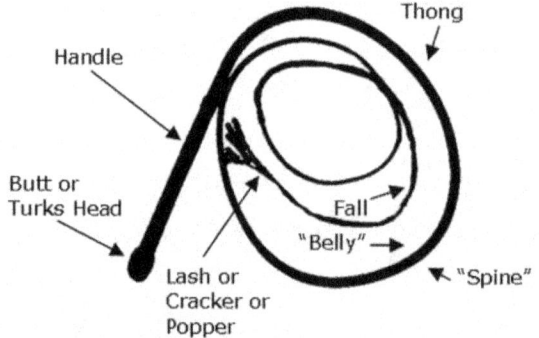

**ANATOMY OF A WHIP**

**Butt or Turks Head**
Knot at end of whip
**Handle**
Long-handled whips are called "Target Whips"
**Thong**
Braided length between handle and fall
**Fall**
Lace from thong to cracker. Easy to replace
**Lash or Cracker or Popper**
String on end of whip that makes noise.
**"Belly" and "Spine"**
Belly is inside curl of whip; Spine is outside curl. Whip wants to roll along this axis.

Every whip has basically the same anatomy: a handle, a tapered thong, a fall and a popper. We'll go into the different types of single-tail whips in a minute.

The inner structure of a whip is more complex than most folks realize. You have a core, sometimes a shot load bag, over that is a bolster (also called a belly)), over that is a braided whip, and over all that is the overlay.

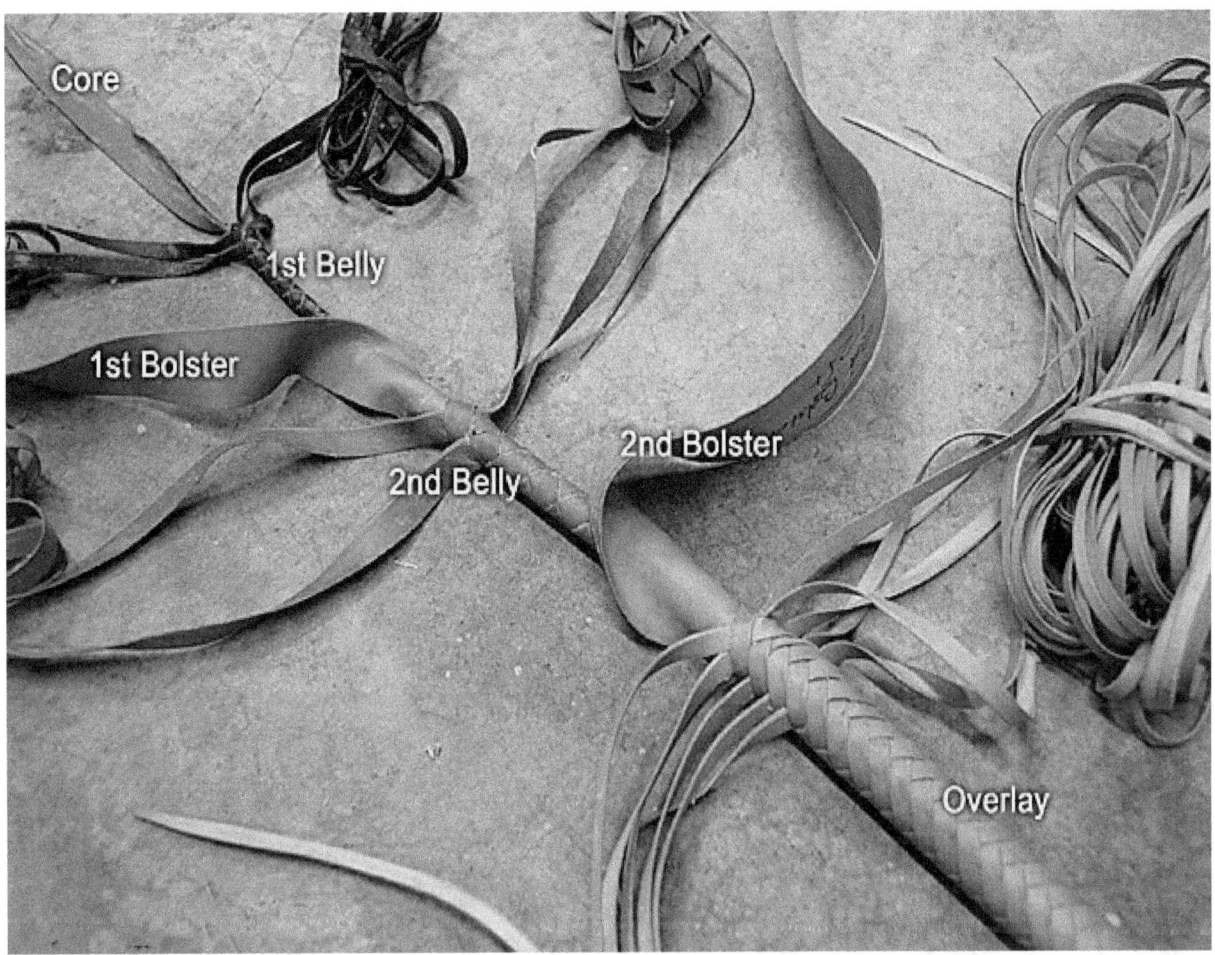

They are braided so they fit snugly against each other. If the whip's strands slip and slide against each other, even between layers, the friction makes the whip lose its energy as the loop rolls down the thong.

I have oversimplified it, because there are many variations on this.

## The Physics Behind It All

All whip cracks (even towel snaps) are variations of one action: As a loop traveling along a thong becomes smaller, the loop's speed increases.

In a whip, the handle transfers the force of the throw into the whip, creating an energy loop that travels along the thong. It is a big rolling circle, from the handle to the popper. Due to conservation of angular momentum this loop accelerates as the size and mass of this loop decreases as it rolls out toward the tip of the whip.

This is also why a whip is tapered (and why you can't throw a rope as effectively as a whip). As the loop moves away from the thrower, there is less mass moving as the whip tapers. This rolling "wheel" of the loop gets smaller as it travels to the popper, and the mass of the tapered whip also gets smaller. To maintain constant momentum, the angular velocity increases rapidly until it reaches the end of the whip, breaks the sound barrier and causes the crack.

It is like an ice skater doing a spin: as they pull their arms in closer to their body, they spin faster and faster.

This is why, when the ever-diminishing loop reaches the end of the thong, the popper breaks the Sound Barrier and "cracks." If you really want to delve into the subject (complex mathematics and all), check out http://www.scientificamerican.com/article/true-cause-of-whips-crack/

You also might want to look at http://www.eurekalert.org/pub_releases/2002-05/aps-wcm052302.php (The actual paper in pdf form is at http://www.e-kaczor.net/keiko/whip.pdf)

**The Real Source of the Whip's Crack**

The power of a whip's crack come from your belly, your "Chi" center, your body's center of gravity. You are the mass behind your whip, because it's not just the mass of the whip going into the throw – it's your mass, as well. You transfer this building power through your arm and hand, and this wave travels through the handle into the whip.

Both sides of Newton's equation ( must be equal. That's why, in reality, you can go slower if you go bigger in your moves. And this is why a shot-loaded whip doesn't need to travel as fast to get the same power (more mass).

You want to feel the whip tug all the way through the shot. This is how poi spinners keep control of their tools. If you let the whip "fall asleep" before it cracks, its energy will dissipate.

In short, you do not have to "muscle" a whip to make it crack. The power is already in the whip. It's a matter of form, not force. You don't make a whip crack, you let it crack.

You will be "riding the horse in the direction it's going." In other words, you get the whip moving, and then you guide it. Nothing fancy here.

## Different Types of Single-tail Whips

In the modern world, there are basically three types of single-tail whips: snake whips, stock whips and bullwhips. Whip cracking technique is only slightly different for each class of whip.

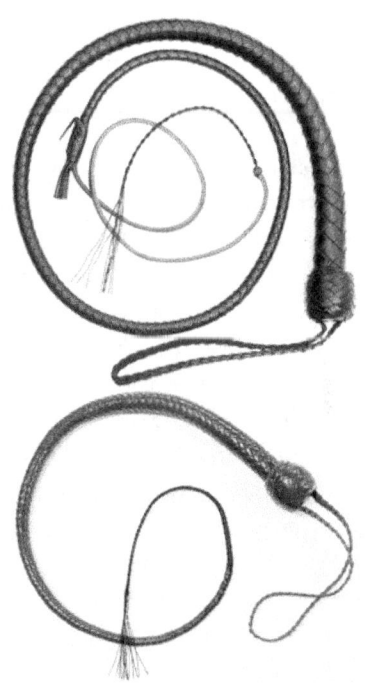

The **Snake Whip** is a short whip with no rigid handle. It is flexible its whole length and has a fall like a bullwhip. Such whips are usually three or four feet long, but some whip makers routinely craft 14-foot snake whips of astonishing grace and accuracy. A snake whip can be rolled up to be stuffed into a pocket or saddlebag. (Historically, these whips also have been used as blackjacks or koshes.)

Another type of Snake Whip is called the **Signal Whip** (also called a dog whip, from the sled mushers of the North). The differences between them are slight but significant: The Signal Whip does not have a fall. Instead, the popper is braided into the thong, so it is one continuous piece.

The **Bullwhip** has a rigid handle, usually 8 to 10 inches long. The thong arises from the handle in a gentle transition. A bullwhip with a longer handle, usually 12 to 15 inches in length, is called a Target Whip.

Bullwhips can be 4 feet or 40 feet long. A comfortable indoor whip is 4-5 feet long,, but you don't get the hang time of a 6-foot or longer whip, which to me is an important part of the bullwhip experience.

There are many different types of bullwhips, a category which may include coiled-wrap whips, chain-mail novelty whips and swivel-handled whips, among others. Some are classified by the material the whip maker uses to create them, such a kangaroo ("roo"), nylon and other flexible and strong material.

I'll take a moment to talk about the swivel-handled whip. The drawback to this whip is the disconnect between the handle and the thong, and the resulting unpredictability of its direction of roll. I have rarely seen one of these whips have a swivel snug enough to not wobble. The whip falls asleep at the transition from the handle to the thong. This type of whip rotates when it is thrown forward, making it more difficult to keep on a straight line. The only advantage this whip has is that it's usually cheap. But a cheap whip is no bargain if you can't get past the limitations of the whip.

The **Stock Whip**, favored whip of Australia, is a flexible thong attached by a knuckle to a long rigid handle 14 to 24 inches long. Thong lengths range from 5 feet to 10 feet and longer. The stock whip's longer handle allows a person on horseback to to crack the whip safely away from the animal. English stock whips had a crook or horn at the end of the handle with which a rider could unlatch a gate without having to dismount.

The stock whip is a big part of Australian culture. County fairs have whip competitions for competitors as young as five years old. The Australians have named and described distinct cracks and combinations to the point that their local and national competitions have objective standards of excellence for scoring routines. The United States competitions I have seen incorporate a lot of what's in the Australian contests. Perhaps these standards will be considered objective enough to allow bullwhip events in future Olympics.

Some Australian stockmen use a "bullocky whip," which is a very long thong attached to a 10-foot pole and is cracked by swinging in the air like a flag. It's a super-sized stock whip.

As a subset of Stock Whips, **Coach Whips** and **Dressage Whips** feature a long flexible handle with a long thin thong ending in a cracker. Because of the handle's length, a fisherman's hand snap is usually sufficient to make it crack. I admit I have seen some whip crackers ho were very accurate with these whips.

To simplify things, think of single-tail whips in three classes:

- **Bullwhips** have a rigid handle and a thong, fall and popper.

- **Snake whips/signal whips** are shot-loaded thongs with no rigid handle, flexible all the way to the butt.

- **Stock whips** are snake whips on a stick.

**Wild West Whips**

Stage coach drivers in the Wild West used to be called "whips." Some of the more famous whips were Buffalo Bill Cody, Wyatt Earp, and Wild Bill Hickok. Another famous whip, Charlie Parkhurst, was found to be a woman after her death.

These days, most whips are seen on ranches, circuses, rodeos, reenactments, and movie sound stages. As the audiences for fire whips and black light nylon whips have increased, more Goth, flow, and alternative lifestyle events feature whips.

In Australia's Outback and in U.S. cattle country, the whip is a working tool. It allows one to safely and effortlessly exert authority at a distance over livestock. No good cattle or sheep drover intentionally hits an animal with a whip, because this would only bruise the meat, damage the hide, and anger the animal. It's the noise that's used, not the impact.

Reb Russell performing in 1937.

## Chapter 2 – A Foundation for Good Whip Cracking

**Get a Good Grip – Belly Up – Creating Safety Zones -
Point and Squeeze – Practicing with Both Hands**

Here's what's ahead for you in this chapter:

- You will be shown how to hold your whip (and why).

- You will be shown how to use the whip's natural shape to your advantage

- You will be shown how to create your "safety zones."

- You will be shown how to make your whip crack where you want it to.

There's your solid foundation for safe and enjoyable whip cracking.

### Get a Good Grip

First, hold the whip correctly. This means the butt of the whip is in the center of your palm. Don't grab the whip halfway up the handle.

Hold the handle so the Turk's head knot on the end is in the center of your palm. Hold it firmly, but in a relaxed fashion. Imagine a ball-and-socket joint.

## Belly Up

A good whip has a natural curve to it, a way it wants to hang. The whip wants to roll along this curl. This curl is caused by the bolster in the whip, called the belly – as a consequence, the resulting curve also is called the belly. The belly is the inside curve of this coil. The outside part is called the spine. Belly-Spine – Got it?

It's your choice to crack with the belly or against it. By this we mean, should you crack in the direction of the whip's natural curve or go counter to it?

The many whip makers I've spoken to agree that it doesn't matter, as long as the whip is rolled out along its belly-spine axis. Personally, I prefer to go with the belly, since the whip will roll out predictably and consistently. When you crack against the belly, you may get a sharper bang because of the percussive spring-back action, but accuracy and control of the whip is lower. Still, it's your choice. Here's how to do it, either way.

### Against the Belly:

Hold the whip out in front of you so it hangs down. Do you see the curl? Turn the handle a little to the left, a little to the right. Gravity will tell you where the belly is.

Gery Deer cracking against the belly

### With the Belly:

Do the same thing as you did above, but give the handle a half-turn in your hand, so the curl is arcing upward, like an elephant's tusk. The whip will curl in a downward arc. The whip will curl toward you and hang down over your elbow. Voila!

From here on, I will assume you are cracking with the belly, only because that is my own preference. But anything I say here can be adapted to let you crack against the belly effectively. Try them both – decide for yourself.

The whip wants to roll with the belly. If you aim the handle down, the whip will make a loop that rolls toward the ground, like "water flowing downhill." Do this a few times. You can predict where the whip will want to to roll.

That's how you control your whip, by using the predictability of the belly to your advantage. Eventually, you will be able to feel in your hand where the belly is, the best way for the whip to roll out, without looking while you are cracking. It can be done by feel.

There are several simple techniques you can use to make sure you know which way the whip wants to roll out most easily. Simply, you hold the whip so it's aligned with the belly: Thumb style or Vee style.

Thumb style is when you extend your thumb up along the handle so you can use your thumb to aim the whip. You'll know where the whip is going without having to look at it. Also, it lets you "pull the trigger" which adds more oomph to the crack.

Vee style is made by by aligning the belly with the V made by your thumb and first finger. Now, when you throw the whip up, down or sideways, you know where the loop will roll most easily on the belly-spine axis. (Don't use your index finger – it makes the whip wobble.) When I am cracking, I switch back and forth as needed.

The whip wants to follow the handle, so if you hold the whip completely straight, it will smack your elbow or your shoulder. To prevent this, turn the whip slightly so the whip drapes outside your arm. Now angle the handle just a bit outside your elbow. When you pull the whip up into a wide circle, if your forearm is straight up and down like an extension of the handle, the whip will pass harmlessly outside your arm.

The flow of the whip comes from your full arm, with a firm but passive wrist. Use a passive wrist, not an active one. You don't crack a whip by snapping your wrist. The power comes from your whole arm, your whole body, not just your wrist.

### Rotating the Whip

Years ago, I was told by most whip makers that you should crack a whip only along its belly-spine axis.
If you didn't, your accuracy would suffer and your whip could get screwed up. The whip was made for this action.

Whip maker Joe Wheeler tells me he's been hearing about folks cracking their whips from all angles, essentially rotating the whip when they use it, working it from the top to the bottom, from side to side.

The reason for this is that the leather at the transition from handle to thong could be weakened by constant use, resulting in a "floppy" whip.

Stretching the leather from all sides when you crack will give your whip a longer life.

He explains that this is a technique to be used gently, when you are cracking just for the sound. (I assume the belly-spine axis remains in play for accuracy.)

A whip cracker will sit with his/her whip and form an arc, rotating it in their hands to work out the tight spots. This is not bending back and forth; it is a gentle stretching and rolling.

Which brings us to how to create Safe Zones so you don't continually whack yourself. Once more, this is a simple visualization exercise.

### Creating Safety Zones

To create safe zones where you will not hit yourself, imagine you are standing in the middle of railroad tracks.

If the whip is outside the tracks and you are inside the tracks, you will not be hit. Keep the whip outside the railroad tracks and it will not strike you in the head or back.

But if the whip comes inside the tracks – in front of you or behind you, at any point – you will be whacked. And if a part of you, like an elbow, crosses the line and goes outside the tracks, that part will be whacked.

Repeat: the whip wants to go where the handle is pointing, so try to keep the handle parallel to your body.

Using this same principle, if you are cracking on a horizontal plain (like with a Cattleman's Crack), make sure your hand is higher than your head – that is, outside the tracks.

Good news – the tracks are on both sides of you. This is how I can throw an Overhand Flick on the right side that sweeps down to my left side, then back up into a backhand that sweeps down to my right side, again. (This is a real swashbuckler's move.)

When you hear the whip crack, the energy is expended. It is now moving from momentum alone, and it is ready to go into another crack, so this can become a continuous multiple-crack move.

**Point and Squeeze**

"Point and squeeze," also called "pulling the trigger," is an energetic and brief squeeze, not an overpowering snap. (This wristless whip technique also will help you avoid Carpal Tunnel Syndrome.)
Just as the whip cracks, squeeze the handle of the bullwhip – just a quick tense – and aim down the Vee or the thumb to tell the whip where you want it to crack. Point it, just like Harry Potter's wand.

For a whip with no handle like a snake whip, the turkshead knot should be held firmly and lightly, with the knob allowed to rotate freely in the hand like a ball-and-socket joint. This will minimize the bending stress near the turkshead knot. Another advantage of the passive wrist approach is that the whole arm smoothly flows with the whip, reducing the likelihood of the whip's braid failing at the point of stress (usually right at the transition between the handle and the thong).

Basically, you want your palm to always face the direction you're throwing the whip. When I warm up without a whip, it looks like I'm doing Tai Chi – but I'm not.

Hand position is vital. I can use the Vee of my hand to help me line up a throw. Even when I am throw a flat sideways crack (like flipping a Frisbee), I make sure my palm faces the way the whip is going to travel.

This principle includes your forearm, which should be an extension of the handle. If I move my arm straight up and down, I make sure my elbow is on the line of vertical motion. The single most common mistake beginners make is to flap their elbows out to the sides as they pull the whip up.

If I perform a 45-degree overhand crack (forward or backward), my hand also is at a 45-degree angle.
If you use the stock whip thumb-along-the-handle grip, the only change is that you'll use your thumb instead of the Vee of your hand to align the whip.

### Practicing with Both Hands

With much patience and practice, you've gotten good with your dominant hand. Now I tell you to put the whip in your other hand and try again. There's a difference, right?

When you try new throws with your off hand, you may feel awkward. You may be embarrassed and self conscious.

And that's fine!

As humans, we learn more from our mistakes than we do from our victories, so I hereby give you permission to make lots of mistakes, because that is how you will learn the most. Cracking with your right and left hands is not the same as two-handed cracking. That is a "hoss of a different hue," as the cowboys say.

Be willing to make mistakes! A practice session is the right place to make mistakes, not when you're showing off or performing.

Here are four great reasons to practice with both hands:

1. It will shorten your learning time because when you get tired with one hand, you can switch to the other. Besides, working both arms builds muscles on both sides. Symmetry is beauty.

2. When you use your dominant hand, you tend to over think. Intellectualizing can get in your way. When you use your off hand, you are less likely to think, focusing instead on what it feels like. You are more in reality and less in your head. You're less likely to compare what's happening with how you think it ought to be happening. In short, you become a child — which is to say, you become teachable.

3. When you get into the moment, you get into your body. Your dominant hand will learn

Paul Nolan not only cracks whips, he makes them.
His whips have been used in many movies.

from your weaker hand. After you've worked for a while with both hands, you may be amazed to see how much your weaker hand has just taught your dominant hand.

4. It is healthy and holistic. You are teaching both sides of your brain, making this an integrated experience. You will learn more completely by educating both the right brain and the left brain. (This is a juggler's trick.)

You can now consciously see things that you do unthinkingly with your dominant hand out of habit. By doing something unusual and different, you see the whip's movement in actual reality. So get out of your head; use your off hand to get into the moment with the whip.

Two-handed cracking is not the same as being able to crack with both hands. It is more complex and requires more practice. You should be able to do a specific throw with each hand before you make the leap into performing it with both hands at the same time. More about that later. amazed to see how much your weaker hand has just taught your dominant hand.

## CHAPTER 3 - THE BASIC CRACKS

**The Circus Crack — The Overhand Flick —
The Cattleman's Crack — The Flip Back**

Good news! Almost every crack you'll ever see is a variation on one of these three basic cracks; The Circus Crack, the Overhand Flick and the Cattleman's Crack. If you can get those three strokes down, you can do just about anything.

So check your clearance, line up the whip's belly, visualize the railroad tracks, take a deep breath, relax, and let's get cracking!

**The Circus Crack**

This is the simplest whip crack to learn.

Remember Newton's Second Law? It said that if you increase any part of the equation (Acceleration=Force/Mass), you will increase the power of the other side.

The Circus Crack doubles the distance the whip travels by going up, curling around in an S-shape without cracking and then coming back down.

Lay the whip out on the ground in front or behind yourself. Swing the whip up into a circular arc like you're swinging a rock on a string. Give it enough oomph to get a good tug from the cracker. Make thip stand out as straight from your hand as possible. Feel the pull of the popper.

Use the upward swing to align your whip. I visualize the popper drawing a dotted line. Make the S higher than your head and bring the whip down in front of you along the same dotted line you made going up. Bring the whip back down slightly under its original track and you will be on mark.

You're making a big circle going up, then a smaller circle going down, so it's one continuous move.

Extend your arm! Keep it straight! Don't just use your wrist. Use shoulder rotation, like a steam engine's drive wheel. Keep your elbow straight until your hand is extended over your head, pointing to about 10 o'clock. At the height of its trajectory, bend your elbow and pull your arm down as you straighten your elbow and extend your hand forward.

If you've lined up the belly outside your forearm, and the handle is parallel to your body, the whip will flow forward past your shoulder without striking you.

The whip will crack close to you, from two-thirds to three-quarters of its length. If you hear two cracks – one behind you followed by one in front – you are "snatching" it forward and back.

The Circus Crack is not two cracks, it is one smooth continuous crack, one motion from beginning to end.

This is the cutting stroke for slicing newspapers. It can also be used for putting out a candle, if you make the crack coincide with the candle's flame.

## Circus Crack Tips

Crack the whip either with the belly or against it, not across it. Hold the whip so the natural curve is coiling either up or down.

You'll see the accuracy is not affected, but the force of the Circus Crack is greater when you crack against the belly. This method is also quicker for numerous consecutive cracks.

On the other hand, the whip unrolls more sensuously when you let it unroll naturally. (Don't forget to give the crack a little extra oomph by pulling the trigger with a quick, firm squeeze.)

Make the motion slow and consistent. Don't go slow, then fast. Make it the same speed going up as coming down. Don't rush the forward throw to snap the whip. There is no need.

You can target fairly precisely with a Circus Crack. Hold your arm almost motionless at the instant of the crack, aiming the handle like a wand at your target. You can aim high, aim directly to the front, or aim low. After the whip cracks, follow through to ground the whip on your whip side, or across your body to the outside of the tracks.

You can train yourself to consistently crack vertically by putting two cardboard boxes on chairs and positioning them about two feet apart. Crack the whip down between the boxes. If your aim is off, you will hear the cracker knock the cardboard. When you've improved to the point that you rarely touch the boxes, move the boxes closer together. Keep doing this a little at a time until you're able to crack cleanly down into a gap of about an inch.

## The Overhand Flick

Set the whip out along the ground in front of you. Turn your palm forward.

Pull the whip back behind you, extending your arm fully straight out. Use enough force to lift the whip into the air behind you. Use enough force to get the whip up to the top of its arc where you'll pause momentarily, then push the whip forward.

At this point, hold your hand stationary to let the whip roll forward until it cracks. Do not sweep down into a circle before it cracks. If it doesn't have a chance to form a loop, it won't crack. After the crack, use the whip's momentum to guide the whip down outside the tracks.

The lesson here is: You can't get there before the whip. Give it the little bit of time it needs to get there with you.

It looks like a capital D on its side. The semi-circle is on the bottom and the flat line is on top. Yes, this move drags the whip on the ground, so go gently (no asphalt!).

The rhythm of the overhand flick is ONE-two-THREE.

The ONE is the low sweep backward as you lift the whip so it lies in a straight line in the air behind you, slightly above shoulder level.

The TWO is the pause of the whip in the air behind you at shoulder level.

The THREE is the push forward from your shoulder.

The whip should be an extension of your arm. Just as the fencer holds the epee straight along the line of his arm, an accurate whip thrower will keep his or her arm straight, using the handle to point directly at the target.

Think of a swimmer: if you paddle only with your hands from your elbows in front of you, you will expend a lot of effort but not get very far. The effective swimmer reaches far forward and sweeps far back. So extend your arm fully. This gives the whip the distance it needs to pick up momentum.

## Overhand Flick Tips

Every crack starts with its setup, before the actual throw begins. You should pull the whip in a straight line. If the whip is curled or coiled, it will try to straighten itself at the beginning of the throw and will slue off as the throw progresses. If this happens behind you, you will hit the back of your head.

Be consistent and think in straight lines. If you pull the whip back in a straight line, you should throw the whip forward along precisely the same line. If you pull back along one line and throw forward along a different line, you are changing the direction of the whip mid-throw, which forces the energy building in the whip to dissipate quickly. You might just as well take a pair of scissors and cut your whip in half, because you are, in effect, cutting the whip's efficiency in half.

The Overhand Flick is a targeting throw which can be used to pop balloons or snuff candles. It can also slice playing cards. To be accurate, throw the whip forward at eye level so you are sighting along the whip's handle.

Hold the whip in front of your body, not out to the side. Try to keep the handle parallel to your body though the whole move. If you were trying to impale a target with a sword by holding it out at your side, you would simply be hoping that you hit the target. But if you sighted along the blade, you'd be more likely to hit your target. It's like aiming a pistol. If you minimize the parallax (the difference between the gun sight and your eye), you will become more accurate.

You'll be even more accurate if you throw slightly downhill, somewhat negating the effect of gravity on the whip.

An underhand forward rising crack is the Overhand Flick, except it comes from below and rises in front of you. It's almost the same move made by a bowler.

The underhand backward crack starts with the whip set in front of you, along a straight line. Flick the whip at a spot behind you. You'll need to put a bit more wrist into this one, so that it cracks behind you and rises up after it cracks. This stroke works better with shorter whips, since long whips being pulled across grass lose a lot of their "juice."

To do a sidearm crack, flip the whip forward with your wrist pointing skyward, the whip passing beside your body. The throw forward is a straight line, parallel to the ground. It's just like flipping a Frisbee sideways, underhanded. After the whip cracks, it will continue to travel to your other side. Because you are throwing sideways, gravity has a greater influence on your whip, causing the line to drop as the whip travels. Experience will teach you how much to compensate so you can hit your target consistently and accurately with a sidearm crack.

Yes, the sidearm crack can be thrown as a backhand. Lift the whip into the air so it is parallel to the ground and extending straight behind your right shoulder. Your arm will be crossing your body, with your wrist pointing at the ground and your elbow parallel to the ground. Push your palm forward (not in a sweeping arc) and point the handle at your target (or at an imaginary point in front of you). After it cracks, continue to sweep your hand out to your other side and ground the whip outside the railroad tracks.

With the Overhand Flick, you send the whip out to its full length. It will crack further away from you than the Circus Crack does.

Remember: keep your palm facing forward so you know where the belly of the whip is at all times.

## The Cattleman's Crack

The Cattleman's Crack is a Circus Crack on the horizontal plane above your head. (This is that wild Catwoman crack.)

The Cattleman's Crack is parallel to the ground. (It could also be called the Overhand Reverse.) This is the crack most often associated with Australians, ranchers and cowboys. The idea is to swing the whip in a big circle above you head, then cut back abruptly in the opposite direction.

This works better if you swing the whip in toward your body, then cut back so you sweep your hand out away from your chest, to make the crack. Use your pectoral muscles with a big sweeping motion using your whole arm, not just your wrist, as if you were politely remove a very wide brimmed hat. (You can do it the other way, but it's more awkward.)

Swing the whip in a wide circle, palm forward, hand higher than your head. Give the whip enough oomph so you feel the tug of the cracker. Make sure your hand (and the whip's trajectory) is above your head.

This crack is associated with the notorious swivel-handled whip, which has little grace and less accuracy because of the wobble where the handle meets the thong. This lack of tightness will result in a loss of energy when you throw the whip. It also means your accuracy will be off, since the wobble will communicate the disconnect into the thong. I've heard people swear they have good swivel-handled whips – but I've never encountered one which could not be blasted into shame by a simple, everyday working whip handled correctly.

## Cattleman's Crack Tips

The easiest way to get the feel of this crack is to ease into it gradually. Do a simple Circus Crack, straight up, straight down. When you're comfortable and consistent with that, angle the whip slightly, say 30 degrees, and cut back on the same angle.

Remember to extend your arm in a broad sweep, giving it enough energy to stay lively all the way into the popper before you cut back. Keep your hand high, at least above your head.

Keep increasing the angle as you get control of it until you are swinging the whip around above your head, parallel to the ground. You'll soon figure out how much energy to put into the whip with your swing in order to keep it on a flat plane – and away from your delicate face!

Tim Kiss gives the whip enough oomph to "stay outside the tracks."

You can use the Vee grip technique to make sure you are pulling the whip back along the same line you threw going out.

After a lot of practice, you'll be able to do it with your eyes closed, feeling where the whip is, where it's traveling and where it's going to crack. You will just plain know it in your being because by this time the whip will have become an extension and expression of your whole body.

This crack will occur pretty close to you. I suggest you go slowly and deliberately to get a clean, crisp crack that won't blow your eardrums as if someone had fired a howitzer next to your head. It takes no skill or knowledge or expertise to swing a whip wildly to make a god-awful bang. Anyone can do that! But to be controlled, precise and deliberate in your cracking is the mark of someone who knows what they are doing.

The Australians developed their well-earned fame of working with stock whips because they needed longer handled whips to roll out and away from the horses they were riding.

It's easier to do this crack with a long-handled stock whip than with a bullwhip, so if you're using a short-handled bullwhip (or snake whip), you've really got to make sure you are holding your hand away from your head in order to make sure the whip's line of travel does not intersect your eyes or ears.

## CHAPTER 4 - THE RIGHT WHIP

What to Look For – Plaits and Braids – Long Whip vs Short Whip – Wrist Loops – The Key to Getting a Good Whip – Caring for Your Whip – Sure, Your New Whip is Stiff

**What to Look For**

If you are in a shop or at an event when you consider buying a whip, pick it up (with permission, of course) and examine it carefully. You don't even have to crack it to see if it's well made. Just move it around to see how it responds.

Check the braiding. Make sure it is consistently tight-tight-tight. If any of the strands of the whip feel loose, or if you feel a great inconsistency down the length of the whip, put it back on the table and move on.

If a whip is not braided tightly, and uniformly, the kinetic energy you roll into the thong will dissipear.

In other words, the whip will "fall asleep" at that point. Even if you are not conscious of this, you will intuitively compensate by throwing harder and faster, increasing the odds that you will ruin your efficiency, reduce the whip's actual power, disfigure the grace and beauty of the whip's flow, wear yourself out faster, and most certainly spoil your whip's accuracy.

Crappy whips have newspaper, rope or other cheap filler for a core. Personally, I don't think it helps a whip to be made out of different materials, such as kangaroo plus paracord. The materials will work against each other and not achieve harmony. A good whip is made of good consistent materials from the inside to the out, layer by layer, until the final plaited overlay. As the Chinese saying goes, "You can't carve rotten wood."

The materials that go into making whips may vary, but the preferred leather is kangaroo ('roo'), because the skin of that marsupial from Down Under is twice as strong as cow leather at only half the weight. This lets the whip maker pull the leather laces strongly to get a tight, snug weave without breaking strands. It results in a whip which is light and lively.

I have seen South African whips made from eland. I have cracked Mexican whips and Russian whips. I have seen whips made of chain mail, rope, rubber, and nylon. I have tied a popper on the tail of a novelty plastic snake and it went off like a shot. For all their differences, all these whips cracked. I have heard of whips made from hippo, elephant, walrus, and other animal skins, but at this writing, 'roo is the preferred material of most whip makers.

You can get a decent whip make of Indian-tanned cow leather or latigo, instead of kangaroo. This will make the whip less expensive, and if the whip maker is a practiced artisan, the whip could compare favorably to its natural hide counterpart. Some whip crackers prefer to use nylon whips for a variety of good reasons. Nylon whips are working tools in wet, swampy areas of Louisiana and Florida. Some colors of nylon glow brilliantly under UV lights, which makes them great for variety stage shows.

To pick the right whip, it helps to know how you intend to use it. For example, if you're going to work cattle, you may want to go with a stock whip. If you are interested in accuracy, you might want to get a target whip. If you are going to use your whip in a claustrophobic urban setting, you may be best served by a snake whip, because it's hard to crack a 12-foot bullwhip on a 10-foot balcony (yes, it can be done).

## Plaits and Braids

When someone says they have a "16-plait" whip, they're talking about how finely braided their whip is. A whip is made from strands braided together. A simple, crude whip may have as few as 4 strands in a round braid. An inexpensive, decent bullwhip can have 8 strands (or plaits). A 12-plait whip is a sturdy, elegantly braided tool which can look beautiful and work superbly. A 16-plait whip is smoother (like snake skin) and made with correspondingly thinner strands. It will be slightly heavier than a 12-plait whip.

Hiram Bingham, the real Indiana Jones.

A 24-plait whip is expensive and requires a master whip maker's expertise, but the finer strands allow the whip maker to do some fancy plaiting, like braiding the whip owner's name into the turkshead knot at the end of the handle, or to weave flowers or other designs up the handle using different colored strands.

I'm seeing more whips being made with metal ferrules like napkin rings around transition points. These can be artfully engraved with serial numbers or the owner's name. Some are quite beautiful.

I have heard of 72-plait whips. Can you imagine a whip maker putting in the hours and days of braiding 72 hair-like strands around and around, pulling them tight, in order to make a whip that is a piece of art? A whip like this should be shown in a glass case, not worked as a practical instrument.

Some whips look like coral snakes, while others may have a purple and black two-tone look which is moody and sharp. I have seen pink whips, gold whips, white whips. If you specify colors or combinations of colors, the price of the whip will be jacked up accordingly.

The more finely braided a whip, the greater the likelihood that a strand could eventually break, requiring a repair job by the whip maker. Frankly, I like 8-plait and 12-plait whips, because the braiding can be fine enough to be consummate, but it's rugged enough to be worked hard.

**Long Whip vs Short Whip**

When someone says a shorter whip is "faster" than a longer whip, this can be misleading. They both crack at the same speed, breaking the sound barrier at 761 mph, but while one whip may achieve this in four feet, a longer whip may achieve this in 12 feet. The 12-foot whip will have a longer hang time, while the shorter whip will get to the crack sooner, since the acceleration to the speed of sound occurs over a shorter distance.

This is what we mean by "faster" – the whip's cycle is briefer.

When Chris Camp throws his 40-foot bullwhip, folks are surprised
to see he can be accurate enough to snuff three candles in a row.

Handling a shorter whip is easier than cracking a long whip because it is lighter and faster, meaning you will not wear yourself out as much in practice. It requires you to use a stricter form, because there is less margin for error. Once you understand a crack and can perform it with some consistency, you can try the move with a longer whip, remembering to allow for the extra weight of the whip and the added hang time.

Working with a long whip is like doing bench presses with one arm. The problem with learning new throws with a long whip is that the extra length allows the whip handler to be sloppy. The pitfall is that poor form may become a bad habit when a whip handler bullies a whip. And that's not the fault of the whip maker.

Further, a short whip is more accurate simply because you're standing closer to your target. But if your aim is off by a half-inch with an short whip, it could turn into a miss of 4 inches in a longer whip by the time the roll goes all the way to the cracker.

**Wrist Loops**

A wrist loop is sometimes braided into the handle. If you put this strap around your wrist, you risk yanking your arm if the whip catches on something. It also gets in the way of doing clean volleys.

The solution to this is to use the loop the way a policeman or fireman would use a baton with a strap: slip a few fingers through the loop and let the whip hang down from the back of your hand. When you turn your hand around to grip the whip, it will be held safely snug and secure in your hand like a ball and socket.

**The Key to Getting a Good Whip**

Know your whip maker.

Pay attention to his or her reputation. Good whip makers become known around the world. Every whip they make is a statement of the level of their craft, so if someone allows you to try one of their whips, this can give you an idea of what to expect from that particular whip maker.

Top whip makers in Australia are often members of the Australian Plaiters and Whipmakers Association (APWA). They monitor business practices to make sure they are ethical, and they offer a newsletter, "The Australian Whipmaker," which gives results of whip braiding competitions.

Then there's is the Australian Whipcrackers and Plaiters Association (AWPA). A different organization altogether. Their mailing address is AWPA, RMB 2925, Wangaratta 3678, Victoria, Australia.

A whip is personal, so as a point of etiquette, never pick up anyone's whip unless they have given you permission to do so. Think about it: How would you feel if you walked out of a store to find someone sitting in your car, "just to see what it feels like"?

Further, if someone gives you the go-ahead to crack their whip, please don't go balls-to-the-wall to see how loudly you can crack it. If someone does this with one of my whips, I take it out of their hands and chastise myself for being the fool who let an idiot potentially damage my whip. Hard cracking is stressful to the fall and popper. (It also annoys people who may be within earshot.)

Using the car analogy again, how would you feel if you let someone test drive your car and they immediately floored the gas pedal and peeled out, smoking rubber up the street? Respect the whip and the whip owner. You don't need to shatter windows to see what a whip feels like.

You can buy from a whip maker by phone or over the internet, but unless it's one of the top-notch makers, be wary of buying sight unseen. A whip can look great in a photograph, but in your hand it may be dreadful. While a recognized whip seller (like Western Stage Props), the fellow who is advertising on Ebay might either knowingly or mistakenly be misrepresenting his whip (Right – an "Indiana Jones" bullwhip for $49.95...O-kay...!).

Of course, even a great whip maker can have an off day. Maybe he had a fight with the wife the day before, or he had a plumbing emergency in the middle of the night, or he drank too much coffee that morning before sitting down to plait a precise and demanding whip. My own belief is that how a whip maker feels gets plaited into the whip. That's one reason why , in my opinion, a good whip maker is a living treasure like traditional sword makers venerated in Japanese culture.

A good whip is a good sword, on many levels. It has a Chi, a life force, which is palpable. The whip feels alive in your hand. You'll know it when you feel it.

I've noticed that different whip makers tend to make whips match the way they throw. Different whip crackers like different whip makers because they are sympatico with that whip maker's style. It is not "one size fits all." Not by a long shot.

Different whips of the same type may have different weights in their shot loading (the amount of weight added to the handle to increase the mass), which translates into a more powerful and percussive throw. Experience will show you your own preference. Some of my own whips have a heavier than normal shot load so I can go slower and still get the power I want. This is helpful when I am doing targeting stunts because I can make my throw more precise and guarantee that I will still be able to slice that banana, for example.

A general good length for a bullwhip or stock whip is about 5 feet long. This gives the sailing hang time experience, but it is short enough that you can practice without burning yourself out in five minutes.

Check prices. A store can jack up the price of a whip deplorably.

That's why I always suggest you deal directly with the whip maker. Most of them are very easy to reach and they love to talk to their clients. If it's a good match between you, you've not only found your whip maker, you've got a new friend!

You may have to stand in line behind the whip maker's other clients, and if the whip is coming from overseas, it may run afoul of some patriotic bureaucrat wearing a Customs uniform who wants to tag on some obscure tariff before you can collect your prize. If you are nervous, go to a reputable reseller. Sure, they are in the business to make a profit, so you'll pay a bit more for your whip, but you'll be more certain of getting the whip you want. It's a tradeoff.

If there's something you especially want in a whip (ie wrist loop/no wrist loop), a whip maker will usually try to accommodate you, from customizing a whip's color scheme, to tinkering with the weight of the shot load, to varying the length of the fall to the length of handle. Don't be afraid to ask. After all, it is your whip, and if you are happy with the result, you'll make the whip maker happy – and you'll have a whip you can keep and enjoy for many years.

**Caring for Your Whip**

Care for your whip the way you care for your car. To keep your car in good running condition, you make sure it has gas and oil and water. You put sufficient air pressure in the tires. When you pull into a gas station, you take a squeegee and clean the windows, mirrors and headlights.

If this is too mundane, compare your whip to a pistol. You'd clean the pistol, oil it, make sure it is not bumped or banged. You'd respect it as an instrument and a weapon.

Should you do any less for your whip?

Watch where you're cracking. I suggest you crack your whip on grass, carpet, or polished floor. Don't crack on sand, dirt or asphalt. Sidewalks and driveways act like sandpaper on the strands.

Try, as much as is humanly possible, to keep your whip off the ground. When you are cracking, only the fall and popper should touch the ground. While this is not always possible (especially with a longer whip), this will save your finely braided thong from being subjected to the abrasions and the ravages of repeated impacts with the ground. This lengthens the useful life of your whip and help it stay in good working condition.

Keep your whip clean. If you get pieces of grit or grains of sand in your whip, they'll work their way between the strands and act like tiny saws every time you crack your whip.

Keep your whip happy with a good leather conditioner. Do not use Neats Foot Oil (it'll burn like gasoline and give the whip an oily, greasy coat).

You should condition your whip when it is feeling dry. The whip is made of leather, which is animal hide. If your own skin gets dried out from wind and sun, it cracks and becomes more brittle. Your whip will do the same thing. Good conditioner works like a moisturizer. This does not harm the whip, if done judiciously.

Most leather conditioners are a mix of bees wax or tallow, lanolin and other ingredients that are healthy for the whip. Condition your whip as needed, not by the calendar. When it feels dry, massage some conditioner into it. Let it sit, then wipe it off with a clean cloth.

Start from the handle and pull toward the popper. Let it soak in for a while and then wipe it off with a clean cloth.

When the whip needs another treatment down the road, you may not have to go all the way up the thong to the handle. Just treat the part that needs it – usually the fall or the end of the thong.

Condition the whip's fall more often than the rest of the whip to keep it supple and pliable. The fall was made to be replaced eventually without requiring the whole whip to be rebraided. Judge by how the fall feels in your hand. If it's stiff, treat it.

The handle itself may not need conditioning at all, and in fact will be better served by minimal conditioning.

(The old cowboys I knew told me the best whip conditioner was the sweat from your own hands!)

Warning: The more you condition it, the more you'll make your whip a dust magnet. Over conditioning a whip weakens the strands, loosens the braiding, and makes your whip a virtual vacuum cleaner for all the dirt, dust and shmutz in the world. Not conditioning a whip often enough results in a whip that's dry. It will not roll smoothly, and the leather may crack and chap, just like your own skin would if you were dehydrated.

The condition of a whip is the result of how vigorously it is used, the humidity, etc. There are no hard and fast rules, only principles which can decide to apply or not. So let the whip tell you when it needs to be treated.

**Sure, Your New Whip is Stiff**

So are you when you get out of bed on a cold morning!

Your new whip will break itself in as you use it. There is no short cut. Some whips come with a shellac coating (nylon whips may be waxed). This will naturally wear off in time.

When you store your whip, coil it gently in the same direction as the belly. You can wind the fall around the loops of the whip to keep it together for storage, but some experts like Andrew Conway suggest this is not good since the fall will be crooked when you unlace it from the whip. Whatever you do, don't tie the thong around itself. You will weaken the whip at that point. I lay my whips sideways on a shelf, stacked, or I place the next to each other vertically like books. I can tell which whip is which by the handle. Store your whips out of sunlight, away from air conditioning, in a dry area.

# Chapter 5 - Improve Style

Setting the Whip — Pulling the Trigger — Foot Position —
Getting the Most Out of Practice — Listening to Your Whip —
Twelve Principles of Whip Artistry

**Setting the Whip**

Setting the whip (also called "grounding" the whip) is a vital skill, for both safety and style. It's a way to remove energy from a whip so that a crack that begins to go wild will not harm anyone. It is a way to line the whip up straight on the ground so the next crack starts clean and pure.

Setting the whip is done by simply flicking the wrist to use the handle to lay the whip out along the ground. The whip wants follow the handle, so point the handle where you want the whip to go.

Setting the whip can be done standing or kneeling. Roll the whip out in front of you by planting the whip into the ground with enough force that the loop continues to roll all the way down the thong. Make it roll out in front of you, then then back, several times, letting the whip roll along its belly-spine axis under its own momentum.

When you roll it behind you, twist your hand around so you are pushing the whip, your palm facing the direction of the roll. You don't want to yank it backward over the back of your hand. The whip will torque around and and end up splaying across the ground in a tangle.

**Pulling the Trigger (Point and Squeeze)**

You'll remember this from Chapter 1. Let your hand hang in the air for a moment after the crack. The result will be crisp, sharp and powerful report.

This is not snapping your wrist to make the whip crack. It's indicating to the whip the precise point where you want it to crack.

If you hear a thick leathery thud with or without the sharp crack from the popper, it means the whip has cracked in the fall and not the popper. You haven't given the crack enough time to travel down the thong to the popper. The whip is telling you to slow down a tad.

You can do this with circus crack or just about any other crack or combination of cracks (a combination of cracks is a "flash," which we'll come to shortly).

You can also momentarily pause a whip during a pass to create a second crack.

This technique also is the secret to doing wraps safely if you perform or play with another person. Want to do an arm wrap? Start with a stick, then work up to doing a wrap around a well-clothed arm.

Champion whip cracker Chris (The Whip Guy) Camp uses the Point and Squeeze technique to perform the thrilling Throat Cut stunt. (Note: this can be dangerous.)

Point and squeeze at a spot slightly above the stick, then allow the whip's fall to wrap around the stick as a matter of momentum after the crack.

If you follow through without pausing at the squeeze point, the fall will slap the stick with enough force to knock it away.

If this happened during an arm wrap, the fall would strike the arm and start to accelerate again at the point of impact, resulting in a tourniquet action. The cracker will hit the skin with enough force to really sting and abrade.

Not following through is the key to doing a stunt like a finger wrap safely.

Remember: The instant after you hear the whip crack, the power is gone.

Use this method when you are popping a balloon. The only difference is that you'll make the point of the crack coincide with the very surface of the balloon and not at some point several inches away, as you would with an arm or finger wrap.

**Foot Position**

You guide the whip with your whole body, even when you don't realize it. The whip takes the message you give it and tries to do exactly what you tell it.

This is why a bullwhip is so single-minded. So you must give it a single message, not many conflicting messages.

Here's how it works:

The whip wants to follow the handle, so make sure the handle is straight. The handle should be an extension of your arm, from your elbow along the same line as the handle, like a sword fighter.

More than that, your whole body communicates itself through your joints and bones and muscles to tell the whip how you want it to crack. The whip picks up these subtle messages from your body position and your foot stance.

There are three foot positions:

5. Whip-side foot forward

6. In line with your shoulders

7. Whip-side foot behind.

Incorrect foot position torques your body around. When the foot opposite your whip hand is forward, you are counterbalanced and can gyre wildly backward and forward. You'll throw the whip across your body from the side. You'll be going in two directions at once, above and below your hips, with your accuracy reduced to little more than a hope that your hand and eye will intersect on the target.

So the rule is, "Foot side, Whip side."

At this point, we should introduce the definition of an Executive: "The Executive exists to make intelligent exceptions to the rules."

You can put either foot forward as long as you do it knowing what will happen. For example, if you want to look dramatic when you crack a whip (like Indiana Jones) for a few moments, twist your body around so the foot opposite your whip hand is forward. You will look like a Marvel Comics superhero, even if you miss your target and strain your back as a result of this position.

**Getting the Most out of Practice**

Warm up, practice, then cool down. Stretch yourself out before you begin and afterward. Wyatt Earp himself said, "Fast is fine, but accuracy is forever."

He was dead right.

Don't rush the whip. Every whip is like a sine wave. It will unroll at its own speed. You need to be patient enough to let the wave go all the way through the whip to the popper. With a short whip, this will happen fairly quickly. With a longer whip, you will have more hang time during which the whip will pick up speed, resulting in a more powerful crack than a shorter whip's with an equivalent throw.

The whip itself will tell you if you are rushing it. Listen to the crack. If you hear a thick thuddy crack, it's because the whip is trying to crack along the fall, not the popper. The whip is telling you that you are rushing it – so slow down! When you hear a clean crisp snap, you have given the whip the time it needs to crack in the popper.

You do not have to throw faster or put more power into it. The energy is already there. Let the whip do its job – don't force it. Be effortless. There is actually more power this way.

Jasamine Jackdaw loves to play with the roses.

So get the throw or routine down without cracks, softly and gently. You can increase the speed and add the cracks later.

Break any new move down into bite-size pieces, small bits. See how each bit works, then move it into the next bit. When you put them all together smoothly, you'll get the continuous flow of a beautiful whip stroke.

And you will be in complete control of the entire movement, from beginning to end. This is the one best thing you can do to ensure your safety, and the safety of those around you. Get the form down, not even worrying about the cracks. You can always add the crack later (with the Point-and-Squeeze technique), but you can't compensate for sloppy form.

Be absolutely single-minded. Commit to each throw completely, making sure that every part of your body, every direction that you point, is along the line that you want the whip to travel. If you are holding the handle out at a 45-degree angle, or if your forearm is pointing out, or if your elbow is sticking out, you are telling the whip you want it to go in those directions. The result is that the whip will flop or flip in the air, perhaps with disastrous (but logical) consequences. You can't blame the whip, because it will always try to do everything exactly as you tell it to do at the same time it tries to combine the energies and achieve equilibrium.

If your whip is doing strange or unexpected things, check yourself, first. If it is not the whip itself (due to shoddy or uneven braiding), it is because you are giving the whip mixed signals. To get a handle on this, slow down, watch yourself closely, try to see where you are giving the contradictory commands to your whip.

Of course, rules were made to be broken (check the definition of the Executive Decision in the last section). You can change directions deliberately mid-crack if you want to achieve a planned effect.

For example, I have seen some whip crackers play Tic-Tac-Toe by sending the whip forward toward a grid and rotating the handle slightly at the end of the crack, right or left. This makes the popper make a mark like a half-parenthesis, pointing left or right. Together, they form the O. The X's are easier to make.

**Listening to Your Whip**

You can give yourself accurate feedback while you are learning to crack. Watch your shadow on the ground to see where the whip in relation to your body.

You can also watch yourself in a plate glass window if you are practicing in a backyard. If you are in a dance studio or dojo, you may have the luxury of being able to watch yourself in floor-to-ceiling mirrors.

Taking a video is helpful only long after the fact, like a boxer watching a film of a past bout. But this is a function of analysis, not experience. The feedback is not immediate and tangible. It is mental, but even this can have value. You'll see yourself as your audience sees you.

Doing this, you my realize you can't crack a black whip in front of a black background or dark trees and expect the audience to see it clearly.

It also helps to keep a notebook, making notes on practice. It not only documents your progress, it will help you keep track of your ideas and observations, which can be heartening if you have an off day.

Make sure you bring water to drink. Working with whips can be mighty thirsty work.

**Twelve Principles of Whip Artistry**

Throwing a whip gracefully, powerfully and efficiently is not merely a mechanical activity. It requires clarity, clear purpose.

The trajectory of the whip is truth. It is as precise as a knife blade, as exact as a scalpel, narrow as a tightrope, even as you hold one end of the whip in the air. A whip is a ribbon of road into the universe.
It is lightning brought to earth, divine fire placed in the hands of men. It is the speed of though, the the reach of possibility, the danger of dancing along death's icy brink. The area within the arc of a whip is sacred space. What moves within is real; what lies without is a dream, a shimmering surface reflection.

Each crack is a jewel, a nova glint of star flash, that flare in the eye of one who loves profoundly, the gleam of the knife point flying toward the breathless magician's assistant waiting against the bullseye of the target.

Given all this, you'd better make sure your head is on straight when you pick up a whip. If you don't, it will quickly remind you that we live moment to moment in a world of logical consequences.

**1. Every day is different – and so are you.** Warm up with the whip and check to see where your head is. If you are tense, the whip will be tense. If you are angry, the whip will be angry. Your precision may vary from day to day, as it will in any athletic endeavor or performing art. Forgive yourself for not being perfect every time. The goal is to raise the lower end of your performing zone, not just to expand the top end. Consistency is the mark of champion.

**2. Remember the basics.** Inside the tracks/ outside the tracks, hand and foot position. Where's the belly? Throwing a bullwhip is a whole-body dance, not just a snap of the wrist or a jerk of the elbow. As T.S. Eliot asked, "How can we tell the dancer from the dance?"

**3. You can't get there before the whip.** Slow down! Don't rush or force the whip. A bullwhip wants to work in a straight line, and it is always striving to achieve equilibrium. All you're doing is giving it permission to be itself. You will help your whip by not getting in its way, in any sense, or imposing your will on it inappropriately. The secret here is to "ride the horse in the direction it's going." Don't muscle the whip.

**4. Get in tune with your whip.** A bullwhip will do exactly what you tell it. If it flops in the air or skews, check yourself. I can guarantee that, if it's not a badly made whip, it's because you are confusing it with contradictory messages. The whip gives back what you have given it.

**5. Develop a healthy sense of humor.** Don't take yourself so seriously. Give yourself permission to make mistakes. Fess up if you mess up, then forgive yourself and move on. Make your mistakes while you are practicing, not during a show or when you are cracking with someone. That's not the time to see if you can do something new or difficult. Make your mistakes on your own time. Get your cracks down cold until you own them. Get to the point where each and every crack you throw is completely your own, not someone else's you're trying to imitate.

**6. Ride the horse in the direction it's going.** After the whip cracks, it is immediately ready to go again, to start a new throw, even as it is flying on from the previous crack. The end of one stroke is the start of a new throw. From the moment you pick up a whip until you put it down, it is a continuum, not a series of disconnected moments.

**7. Do not EVER underestimate the danger of a misthrown whip.** Control your environment, from ceiling fans and fire sprinklers to objects on the floor. Brushing against something in the middle of a move will throw the whip off slightly, and by the time it reaches the popper, that discrepancy will be magnified.

If your whip is deflected half an inch behind you, that half-inch can turn into 12 inches when the wave reaches the popper. That could be bad news for a whip cracker or assistant. Because if something can screw up, it will, at some point, and that means it can hurt you or someone else. Expect this and plan for it by giving yourself a margin for error. Err on the side of caution.

**8. Think big.** A whip magnifies your motion, focuses energy. If you go big, you can go slow, and that will give you more control. Give the whip a chance to crack by using your whole arm, extending the whip to its full length to pick up momentum. Once again, we remind you that a good crack starts with a good layout, not with the throw itself. You can't compensate for a partial throw by snapping your wrist. Use a passive wrist. You can add power by squeezing the handle to

Whip cracker

Whip cracker

Whip cracker

Whip cracker

supercharge the throw in the milliseconds before the crack.

**9. Relax your ass.** No kidding. It's a dancer's trick. When you relax your buttocks, you relax your whole body. Try it yourself. Relax your derriere. Keep breathing, slowly and deeply. Don't think about anything except what you are doing.

This is where whip cracking is like the traditional Tea Ceremony in which conversation is limited to the tea, the weather and the ceremony itself. Nothing else is allowed to be discussed. This prevention of extraneous distraction gets the tea drinker out of his or her ego and focuses on the moment, beautifully and calmly. Reality is.

**10. Always perform before your level of capability** until you are well versed in a move or routine. Especially if someone else is in the act.

**11. Own your routines and tricks.** You make them yours only by practice. Don't worry about making the whip crack in the beginning. Get the form down. Move it out of your head and into your body, like a dancer or athlete. You can always add the cracks later.

**12. There is no such thing as throwing a whip** - It's actually **whip pushing** and **whip pulling**. You guide the whip, you don't force it.

If you don't see the value of these principles right now, you will down the road. For now, take what you can use. Come back to it later to see if anything has changed, because this will show you when your own perspective has changed. It's a truism that you don't know what you don't know. The limits of your understanding determine how much you will understand when someone speaks to you from the future. Leave the doors open.

There is no short cut, but you will get there. Pick the whip up consciously and crack it for a few minutes every day. This works better than if you cram a lot of cracking into two hours once a week.

## Chapter 6 - Poppers

*Making Your Own Poppers – The Double Twist Method – The Chopstick Method - Knotting Your Popper – Variations - Attaching Your Popper – Dante's Favorite Attachment Knot*

Poppers can sell for as much as $3 each, but you can easily make your own, as many as you want, for pennies.

The advantage is that you can tailor your poppers for different purposes. You will have more direct control over how the whip functions.

Whips did not always have poppers, but the whips cracked, just the same. According to Andrew Conway, the oxford English Dictionary says the earliest reference in print to a "cracker" or "popper" was from the 19th Century.

The Oxford English Dictionary has some definitions and references which put the terms into historical perspective (I'd like to thank Andrew Conway for these references):

**Cracker:**
An attachment to the end of a whip-lash by which a cracking sound can be produced. U.S., Austral and N.Z.
1835 Monett in J.H. Ingraham South-West II. 288 To the end of the lash is attached a soft, dry, buckskin cracker. So soft is the cracker, that a person who has not the sleight of using the whip could scarcely hurt a child with it.
1880 A.A. Hayes New Colorado (1881) x. 140 Each wagoner must tie a brand-new cracker to the lash of his whip.
1890 R. Bolderwood Col. Reformer I. Xviii. 110 Stockwhips garnished with resplendent crackers.
1907 W.H. Koebel Return of Joe 164 Fresh and efficient crackers swung continually at the ends of the stockwhips.
1966 J. Hackston Father Clears Out 64 I'd plaited a whip specially for the occasion with a new green cracker on it.
**Snapper:**

U.S. A cracker on the end of a whip-lash. Also fig., a sharp or caustic remark.
1817 J. Sansom Sk. Lower Canada 15 One had proposed to put a snapper on the driver's whip.
1841 Knickerbocker XVII. 277 All the whips were provided with red snappers.
1882 Pentecost Out of Egypt iii. 60 She brought out the last end of the question like the snapper on the end of a whip.
1890 O.W. Holmes Over the Teacups xii. If I had not put that snapper on the end of my whip-lash, I might have got off without the ill temper my antithesis provoked.
1903 N.Y. Even. Post 29 Sept 8/2 Senator Carmack is simply adding a snapper to the lash of his vigorous denunciation of the whole Philippine Policy.
1949 B.A., Botkin Treas. S. Folklore iv. 117 Showing off his prowess, he first split a horsefly into pieces, then tore a bumblebee into shreds with the snapper on the end of his whip.

**Popper:**
(The snapper on) a whip-lash. U.S.
1870 Great Trans-Continental Tourist's Guide (rev. ed) 27/1 How often the sharp ring of the popper aroused the timid hare or graceful antelope?
1877 H. Ruede Sod-House Days (1937) The lash is about 1-1/2 inches thick at the handle, and tapers to the popper, and a good hand will make them crack like a pistol.
1933 Amer. Ballads and Folk Songs 375 And the stage driver loves the popper of his whip.
1935 [see bull-whip (bull n. 11)]

**Making Your Own Poppers**

The popper is the most expendable part of the whip. Poppers wear out or fly off their falls with amazing regularity. If you know how, you can quickly replace your own popper without having to wait for the new ones to arrive from the whip maker.

And, of course, making your own poppers is less expensive than buying them from someone else.

It's no big deal, really. If you can tie your own shoelaces, you can make your own poppers.

Experience will show you what kind of popper you should use for what purpose. The choices can be daunting, but nowhere is the pattern for an ideal popper written in stone. It is your choice.

Just as your whip itself should be braided tightly, the popper should be twisted as tightly as possible to make sure the energy of the throw is fully carried to the end of the whip and is not lost in the jostling of loose popper threads at the last moment.

The length of the popper also will now be in your control. A shorter popper is less likely to tangle on the fall than a longer popper will. I prefer long poppers for precision wraps.

You also have more control over the length and fuzziness of the fluffy bit at the end of the popper. A thicker fuzz will act like an air brake, slowing the cracker down. A thin fuzz will be sharp and increase the cutting potential of your popper, making it more like a knife blade.

You can tune your cracker, as whip maker Peter Jack says. By experimenting, I've found I get the best results by making my poppers' fuzzy parts a little longer than normal. I then separate the end fuzz into two strands and snip off one twist so it's half the length of the other part of the fuzz. I rub the popper between my fingers so the strands interlace. This two-lengths-in-one popper gives me both the thick bang I want and the crisp, clear crack of the longer thinner strands at the same time. It makes a two-note chord.

You can make poppers from just about anything. My own preference is mason's twine. It comes in a variety of colors, is readily available and is cheap. Get it from your local hardware store. Make sure it is the twisted mason's twine and not the braided kind!

## Popper Making: The Double Twist Method

Start by playing out a 3- or 4-foot length of thread from a spool across your lap. Without cutting the string from the spool, start back the other way so you now have two strands lying on your lap. Do this as many times, back and forth, as you want. I vary the number of original strands from 6 to 12.

Note: the popper will be ¼ of the length of your original string and 4 times as thick.

Bunch the strands together to make a single string. Pull it tight from both ends. Find the center of this length.

Drape the strand over a hook or nail at this center point and pull it tight. Holding the two ends, twist them in same direction between your fingers. As you tighten them, the strings will begin to resist and try to knuckle over themselves.

Begin rotating and laying the strands over each other in opposite directions. For example, if you are twisting the strands clockwise, lay them over each other counter-clockwise.

Keep the tension tight as you snug the strands up. You will see the spiral of the growing cracker begin to work its way down the string from the nail.

When you have the length you want, hold the strings tight from 3 to 6 inches and make a simple overhand knot to hold the spiral intact. Snip the loose end about an inch and a half from the knot. (There are other ways to tie this off, but this is the simplest.) This will be the part that frizzes out to make the feathery end of the popper. The more strands you started with, the fuzzier it will be.

You want to make sure the popper is braided as tightly as you can get it. If it is loose, it will parachute in the air and flop. It will not carry the force of the crack all the way through the fall to the end of the popper. You will wind up compensating by throwing harder and faster, unnecessarily.

### Popper Making: The Chopstick Method

This is faster than the double twist method. Start by laying out a 3- or 4-foot length of thread on a spool over your lap. Lay out 6 to 12 strands. Don't worry about how skinny it looks. The finished popper will be four times as thick as the combined relatively thin strands you now see draped across your knees.

Using a smooth chopstick, lift the strands up from their center so both halves drape over the chopstick.

Sitting, place the chopstick between your knees so you can pull the strings tight. Pinching all the strands between your fingers as a single thread looped around the chopstick, begin spinning the strings together in one direction. Keep going until the coiled thread is so tight you can't turn it one more time.

Short Cut: I like to make a circle of spiraled string. Through the loops at both ends, I put one chopstick each (so I suppose we could call this the two chopstick technique). The advantage of this is that I can spin one chopstick while the other remains stationary. It saves wear and tear on the finger joints and gives me a nice tight braid.

Pulling tightly with your right hand, pinch that string halfway down with your left hand. Pull outward. Take the right end with the loose strands and fold it back over the chopstick. The string is now doubled back on itself.

With the fingers of your left hand, give the coiled spring a slight spin in the direction it already wishes to travel, and release it. Boing!

The spring action of the twined string will cause the string to ravel together all the way up to the chopstick as a single thread, tightly coiled. Don't let go with your right hand – hold the chopstick and the end of the string.

With your left hand, pull the strung string out and tie a simple overhand knot about two inches from the chopstick. You can now release the loose string at the chopstick end without losing the spiraled string of the cracker. Snip the ends of the strings at the chopstick.

## Knotting the Popper

A simple overhand knot is usually sufficient to secure the popper, but if you want to, you can tie

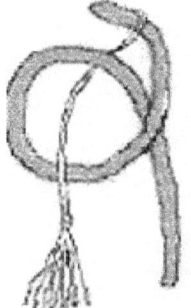

# TO TIE A LASH ONTO YOUR WHIP
## (Aussie Style)

1. Open up the non-fuzzy end of lash.
2. Stick fall through lash end. Snug it in.
3. Make loop in fall. Poke lash through.
4. Pull tight - make self-tightening knot.

each strand off one at a time. This takes forever.

So I like to do a double hitch with half of the popper's string around the other half. This makes the cracker look prettier, giving it less of a noticeable knot before the feathery end of the popper. It's a little more aerodynamic, too, but it's your choice.

## Variations

While you are laying the string out across your lap, you can spice things up by doing a few things. Add some differently colored strings. This will give you multicolored spiral-wound poppers.

You lay a single strand of filament fish line alongside the other strands before you begin twisting. Avoid thick mono-filament line. You want a string that will stay coiled with the other strands. This makes a dreadful cutter, increasing the odds your balloon pop will go off without a hitch.

Poppers can be made of thread, fishing line, horsehair, Kevlar, twine, silk, nylon, dental floss – Just about anything that can be twined. The material used to make the popper can result in a big difference in the sound, both in volume and clarity. Cotton will be muffled, compared to nylon (you might want to make muffled crackers if you don't want to disturb your neighbors). Nylon is sharp. Silk is even keener, but the material has a shorter lifespan. Hair from the tail of a horse is traditional and gives a clean snap. I've been pleased with using plain baling twine. Embroidery thread also is marvelous!

A fat popper made from a soft, thick string will thud more flatly than a skinny popper, which will crack sharply. The choice is yours.

## Attaching Your Popper

There are as many ways to attach a popper to a whip as there are ways to make a popper. If you have a signal whip in which the popper is braided into the end of the whip, you can skip this part. But if you're like most other whip crackers, this is something you really need to know.

With a Texas bullwhip, the process is simple: stick the end of the popper through the slit in the end of the slapper-like fall. Thread the popper's fuzzy end through the loop in the cracker to make a lark's head knot. This will hold.

Here's how you do it like the Aussies:

### Aussie knot

Open the loop in the end of the cracker.

Coil the end of the fall over itself without pushing the end through the loop. Press the end of the popper through the loop and start to snug it up. The knot will tighten every time you crack the whip and should not work loose. After this knot has been in the whip a while, it may become hard as a rock and be impossible to untie. With knots like this, your only recourse is to snip off the end of the fall with the popper. Thank goodness the whip maker sends his products into the whip with a healthily long fall!

With practice, you'll know how much of a nub to leave on your fall. You will want to make the nub as small as possible so the popper does not touch it as it passes over the fall during cracks and volleys.

**Dante's Favorite Attachment Knot**

This is a good knot to use to make the fall-popper transition smoother. First, attach the cracker by making the knot diagrammed above. What you're going to do next is to straighten out the fall so the cracker makes a hitch around the straightened fall.

There is no large knuckle-like knot between the popper and the fall, but you should make sure the popper is twisted tightly into the fall, really biting into it. It will still be easy to remove and replace once you work it loose by "breaking" the knot.

Roll the knot over the end of the popper so it unrolls itself. The popper at the loop will now be tied twice around the fall, overlaying itself. Here again, every crack will tighten the knot, but this time the transition from the fall to the popper will be smoother and straighter. Practice will tell you how close to the end you should tie the popper.

The downside is that the knot really has to bite into the fall, potentially weakening the fall at this point. This knot is more likely to blow the end off your fall. It's a trade off.

## Chapter 7 – Single Whip Routines and Flashes

SI

ow Figure 8s – Fast Figure 8s – Cow and Calf –
Snake Killer – Flourishes – Pausing the Crack – Coachman's Crack –
Volleys – Arrowhead – Plane Variations

Working with a single whip is a great way to learn a new throw, using first one hand, then the other.

Some cracks are more accessible with one hand than with two, such as the Arrowhead or the Self Wrap (see Flourishes). This does not mean they can't be done with two hands, only that it is more difficult.

All the cracks you will ever see are based on these Basic Cracks. Don't worry. It is all within your reach, if you are patient and persistent. You are not learning new cracks so much as you are learning new ways to do cracks you already know.

### Slow Figure 8s

Start with a slow forward Circus Crack. After the whip cracks, continue to swing it in the direction it's traveling, sweeping it beside you in a vertical circle rising behind you. The momentum of the follow through becomes the setup for the reverse Circus Crack.

When the whip is overhead and traveling forward, pull the handle backward so you form the Reverse Circus Crack's S-shape. Remember to reach with your whole arm and not just your wrist.

Make sure the line of the whip is straight up and down beside you and the handle is parallel to your body, or the whip will hit you (see "Inside the Tracks/Outside the Tracks").

After the whip cracks, continue to swing the whip down, then forward and up in a wide vertical circle rising before you. This becomes your setup for your next crack.

Repeat the sequence, forward, back, forward, back. This combination of forward and backward Circus Cracks is called the Slow Figure 8.

These cracks will be slow and lazy, so you'll have time to focus on grace and precision of movement.
Tip: Point your palm toward the direction the whip will roll, so the belly is always lined up with the throw.


### Cow and Calf

This Australian crack is called the Cow and Calf because it is two two cracks – one high, one low (one for the tall cow, one for the short calf).

Throw the whip forward with an Overhand Flick. After it cracks, follow through below so you are pulling the whip into a horizontal position behind you.

Here's the tricky part. Flip the whip forward now with an underhand throw so it cracks as it's rising. After it cracks, the momentum of the rising thong becomes the setup for the next Overhand Flick, coming down. Up and down, each crack occurs at the forward end of the throw.

The **Whoosh Bang** is related to the Cow and Calf, but you start with the calf bringing the whip up after it cracks to throw it back down into a circus crack. (I suppose you could call the Whoosh Bang the "Calf and Cow"!).

Change the plane so the whip is swinging at a 45-degree angle going over your head, and it is now called the **Cross Up.**

Tip: Remember use your hand to line the belly up when it's both rising and coming down. Point your palm toward the direction the whip will roll so the belly is aligned with the roll.

**Snake Killer (Drum Roll)**

This one goes straight up and down with the whip making single crack on the ground in front of you. The trick is to not whack the earth but to time the crack so it's only the popper that touches the dirt.

And guess what? It's also called the Drum Roll when it's done continuously with two whips. It's much more easily done with a stock whip than a bullwhip, but it can be done.

**Flourishes**

My late friend Brian Chic was particularly proud of his flourishes. He invented a self-wrap when he was 12 years old, and he lived long enough to see its authorship claimed by other whip crackers who'd learned it from him. With a slight move of his hand, the whip would dance into a circle, sometimes cracking, sometimes not, but always creating a curlicue of grace and power in the air before he launched into his next sequence of moves.

Flourishes are nice because they are unexpected. They embody the idea that a whip looping back on itself will crack if the loop is tight enough.

This is how the great English whip cracker Vince Bruce would crack a 50-foot whip. He'd lay the whip out in a straight line on the ground, then take a running start and throw a huge loop into the whip, rolling it down the thong. By the time the loop reached its full length, the popper would come up and crack back at him. He was able to do this so consistently that he could hold a target and have the whip cut it when it finally cracked.

I've seen Chris Camp (the Whip Guy) roll out a 40-foot bullwhip precisely enough to snuff three candles in a row. He just knows where it's going to crack.

A fancy flourish is a great way to start a whip cracking routine from a standing start. Lay the whip out in front of you along the ground. Pull the whip overhand into the air toward your hip so that you form a small tight vertical circle beside you at waist height. Continue the trajectory underhand, forward and up. The whip will crack at your waist even as you are lining the rising whip up for your next crack (a circus crack?).

You can do the same crack from the rear: lay the whip out straight behind you. Pull it forward at waist height, palm forward, then pull the handle backward under the line you set up. The whip will crack as it changes of direction to head backward, here it will crack again. Its trajectory now has it rising from the rear, and you are in position to start a new set of cracks.

**Pausing the Crack**

Curious things happen if you pause a whip in mid-crack. When you pick up speed again, the whip cracks at the point of the pause. You wind up with an extra crack in the arc before the final crack at the end of the pass. (This is a variation on the Point and Squeeze technique.)

Whenever a whip cracks, it expends its built up energy - but that is also the moment when it is ready to begin the next crack.

You can play with this, like doing a three-crack circus crack. Perform the circus crack in the normal fashion. This time, instead of a one-two-three beat, perform it has a one-two-three-four rhythm. You'll get a syncopated galloping rhythm.

Adding a pause to the timing stops the handle so the momentum continues to carry the thong without actually falling, then picking up the stroke again.

At the point of the pause, the whip cracks again as it begins to accelerate anew. This will happen whether it's horizontal, vertical, or at any point in between.

Remember that the whip will start to fall on itself before you pick up the motion again. It will crack there. It will also likely crack at the end of the trajectory before you crack it forward, resulting in three cracks.

I can add several such pauses to make the whip sputter and pop up to six times along the arc of an ordinary circus crack. Aussie John Brady can swing the whip in a wide circle around himself while rapidly jerking his hand up and down, the whip making a small crack at the tip of each wave. He calls this the Ocean Wave.
The danger is that if you let it pause too much, you'll hit your own hand. And this is a shot that smarts, for sure. You also need to make sure the pause and pick-up are immediate and take place along the same plane, or you are going to really whack yourself.

As a variation, you can do side arms back and forth with two whips (windshield wipers) with a paused crack to create an interesting beat.

**Coachman's Crack**

This is called the Coachman's Crack because Victorian coachmen used it to crack whips without striking their horses. The whip cracks behind you as it flies forward and up.

This is best performed with a 6-foot whip. You could use a longer whip if you were standing on a platform (or if you had a long-handled coach whip) with a sheer drop-off beside you (like a wagon or carriage).

Begin with a Circus Crack, but pause to let the whip travel further behind you. Have your elbow pointing toward the sky. When the whip goes all the way down it will "bounce" and the popper will rise in front of you. At this precise point, just as the popper stalls in the air, snap the whip handle skyward and straighten your arm fast. As the loop passes over itself, it will crack right beside your ear as loudly as a gun.

This crack can be done with a signal whip or a bullwhip, but it is most easily executed with a stock whip, thanks to the longer handle's greater acceleration.

Tip: Mike Murphy suggested I keep my elbow tightly aimed at the sky, and to wait longer than I thought necessary. It worked for me, so try it yourself.

This is a nice crack to do behind your back as you face the audience. The whip coils around behind you like a snaking halo, and the bang goes off right behind your head. Watch your elbow position and push sharply as the whip picks up speed again.

**The Hungarian Pig Drover's Crack**

Andrew Conway can be credited for naming this paused crack, shown to him at the 1994 International Jugglers' Association annual festival in Burlington, Vermont. He learned the crack from a man who said he'd learned it from a Hungarian Pig Drover.

Swing the whip in a continuous circle on a flat plane over your head, counterclockwise if you're using your right hand. When the whip is out to your side, stop the motion of your handle and let the thong continue to move. After it lags for just a moment, speed your hand up to overtake the thong. As the whip picks up speed again, it will make a second crack.

Watch your hand with this one. The first crack will be coming at you so make sure you move the handle outward firmly and quickly. Don't jerk it. The form makes the crack, not the force.

**Flashes (Multiple Cracks with a Single Whip)**

A Flash is a showy way to crack a whip. Some names derive from the geographical area where the crack originated, like the Tasmanian Cutback.

Before you tackle any Flash, make sure you have good understanding of the basic three cracks and the technique of setting your whip on the ground. You can't run safely before you can walk, so trying to do any of these moves without fully knowing the fundamentals will only teach you sloppy technique and possibly put you (or others) in harm's way.

This is a good place to remind you about wearing that big hat and donning those safety glasses!

Start slow. Don't worry about the cracks. Get the form down first. You can add the cracks later.

Here's where an experienced whip coach is an asset, helping you to experience what a good crack feels like.

Remember – if your form is correct, the whip will almost crack by itself. You don't need to muscle the whip to make it crack. If you do, it's a sure sign you are compensating for bad form.

**Fast Figure 8s**

You learned Slow Figure 8s are basically forward Circus Cracks followed by reverse Circus Cracks. The style is slow.

Fast Figure 8s are a little more complicated. They are very wristy.

Throw a Circus Crack. After it cracks, "bounce" the popper backward, letting it pass over the top of your hand. In other words, you throw the whip forward and then set it behind you before it hits the ground. You'll have a vertical crack forward which immediately rolls into a vertical crack behind you. The is no pause between the two cracks. When repeated, Fast Figure 8s are the bases for Volleys.

### Queensland Flash / Sydney Flash / Victoria Flash

There is little difference between these three-crack Flashes. Each one is a a Fast Figure 8 started with a Circus Crack or Overhand Flick and finished with a rising underhand crack.

The downward arc of the whip as it comes back to you (and cracks behind you) becomes the upward rising setup for the third crack. Crack it in front, then behind, then again as you lift it up. The Point and squeeze technique will ensure a good third crack.

The Sydney Flash is the Queensland Flash with this difference: instead of starting with a Circus Crack, you begin with an Overhand Flick. This one is more difficult to do continuously, because your whip has to stop and change direction from the rising arc after the third crack.

The other reason these cracks have different names is that a different city or state in Australia has claimed the sequence as their own. For example, the **Southern Cross** and the **Queensland Crossover** are almost the same, but you would not call it the Southern Cross in Queensland.

Here's the How: Hold the handle upright, parallel to your body. When people start to throw backward, they usually angle the whip handle out to 45 degrees, but this will make the whip want to gyre backward at an awkward angle as the whip torques. Remember: a crack starts in the setup, not just the execution. So start it out straight.

### Volleys

Now we're into the meat and potatoes of whip cracking!

A Volley is created by simply cracking the whip back and forth, so that every crack becomes the originating point for the next crack. A classic Volley is really a series of Fast Figure 8s.

You can start a Volley with a Circus Crack or an Overhand Flick. The key is to keep the handle almost straight up and down.

That's right – I said "almost straight up and down."

You will have the angle the whip slightly so the thong passes outside your hand instead of whacking it. If you angle it too much, the whip will be working against the belly and skew around in the air.

Crack forward, then back, then forward again, making it a three-crack sequence. After the third crack, draw your hand down in into a circle coming back up, ready to throw forward again into the next three-crack sequence.

Now try it with your other hand. (You knew I was going to say that, didn't you?)

**Variations on a Volley**

I like to throw in Volleys when I'm performing. While the usual Volley has all the cracks occurring above your head, sometimes I will throw in an underhand move. It is dramatic because it changes planes for a moment, but it does not alter the rhythmic snap-snap of the Volley beat, and you can move right back into overhand Volleys without interruption.

When I throw an underhand move to the back, I keep the handle pointed downward after the crack behind me. I pull my elbow in tight to my side. I will need to bob my body slightly to get out of the way of the whip. The whip flies behind my wrist going forward at about waist height. Keep your palm facing the rear! (Yes, you're pulling the whip over the back of your hand, breaking my rules. Remember the definition of Executive Decision?)

Immediately after the whip cracks rising in front of you, begin to lift your elbow up in order to get the leverage you'll need for the next move (and to move your arm out of the way of the returning whip's trajectory). Crack the whip backward, rising. After it cracks behind you, you are now in position to resume the overhand Volleys.

Essentially, you are doing an Overhand Flick forward into an Underhand Flick behind, back into a rising Underhand Flick forward. When it cracks at this point, you are already into the first crack of your overhand Volleys, again.

Because of the awkward connecting angle of the bones of your arm, you need to get that elbow out of the way when you pull the whip backward under your arm. Keep the palm of your hand pointing backward. Make sure you draw the whip to the front along the same line it had going into the crack.

When you draw the whip forward from the rear, make sure you're holding the whip's handle vertically, even though the butt of the handle is above the whip. Push far forward, so the whip extends all the way out to crack before resuming the overhand Volleys in the normal fashion. There, that wasn't so hard, was it? (Oh, did I warn you to wear safety glasses and a wide-brimmed hat?)

**The Arrowhead**

This is a showy move, and it's fun to do. It's pretty close to rope twirling, for a rodeo skill.

Another name for the Arrowhead could be "The Changing Planes Volley." It's easier to perform with a stock whip because the longer handle lets you pivot the plane more easily. With a bullwhip's shorter handle, you have to exaggerate the crossover, really extending your arm across your body.

Let's give it a try.

Start with a simple classic Volley on your right side. Don't rush it.

Tip: Aim at same point directly in front of you from both the right side and the left side. This is the point of the Arrowhead.

Immediately after the whip cracks in front of you, flip the handle as you would if you were setting the whip. Aim the whip to come by you on your left side, handle parallel to your body, very wristy. Reach to compensate for crossing your body. In effect, you are now executing a Reverse Overhand Flick on the side opposite your whip hand.
After the whip cracks behind you on the left side, flip the handle forward again and push the whip forward, aiming for that invisible point in front of you. The whip will crack again. Draw the whip back on your right side as you would in a regular Volley.

Tip: You can work up to the Arrowhead by doing Slow Figure 8s, then Fast Figure 8s while alternating on which side of your body the crack behind you falls.

Remember to keep the whip handle absolutely vertical, if you can. If you angle the handle when you cross your body, the whip will tangle on you. You want the lines of the whip's arc to be perpendicular, whether it's on the right side or the left side.

Try to "bounce" the whip as you do in a Figure 8 or a Sydney Flash. The moment the whip cracks, the thong is still taut, and you are set up to do your next move. You need to be firm, but you do not need to force the whip. There is a difference, and the Arrowhead will show you that distinction.

Don't completely follow through at the points of the Arrowhead. Aim and pause, giving the whip a chance to crack on a straight line, preparing to reverse the whip's direction. Try to keep the whip on a vertical plane, or it will hit you from behind.

If you are a performer, mix it up with a regular Volley and it will look like you're taking a wild ride - but you are still in complete control of the whip.

The second way to do this is to start the Arrowhead in the normal fashion. After the whip cracks in front, you'll pull it back to crack behind you on the left side. This is where the change occurs. When you flex the handle to pull the whip forward, don't aim for that imaginary point in front of you.

Instead, keep the line of the whip vertical and outside the tracks on your left side. After the whip cracks, flex the handle again to pull the whip past you on the left side. In effect, you are doing a brief volley on your left side with your right hand.

Tip: Go slow in the beginning. The form is all important, and you are working out a lot for what looks like a relatively simple move. It isn't so simple, obviously, but it can be done, and done gracefully.

I saw Mexican whip cracker Felix Lopes perform this move at a Wild West Arts Club convention in Las Vegas, and the man epitomized grace and power. I would have sworn I was watching it in slow motion.

This is a form worth striving for.

## Four Corners

This is a Changing Planes Volley that looks like an elevated Arrowhead.

A flat Volley is thrown above your head.

When it cracks in front, pull it back on the flat plane so it cracks behind you, then continue the move into a flat volley again on your left side. There are two cracks in front, two behind - that is, half on the right, half on the left. Keep your wrist aimed at the sky. You'll need a lot of wrist strength to get those four cracks off.

**Hassett's Four Corners** (or **"Four Pointer"**) is named after famed Australian whip cracker James

Hassett, who was a true artist with a whip. The theory is that the whip cracks four times, once for each point of the compass.

**Wells Fargo Flash**

Stagecoach drivers were once called "whips." Andrew Conway describes a particular flash used by stage coach drivers for Wells Fargo & Co,, which started running a cross-country route in the USA in 1858. Twice a week, coaches left St. Louis for the 25-day, 2,757 mile trip which ended in San Francisco at a gallop.

Essentially, this flash is a series of continuous Arrowheads of up to six cracks – one for each of the horses in the team. Folks in distant towns could recognize which stage line was coming in by the pattern of the cracks.

**Helicopter**

The single-handed Helicopter is the Coachman's Crack on a horizontal plane above your head. The trick is to pause the handle of the whip so the thong continues to move before you reverse the throw. If you cut back correctly, the whip will crack behind you.

After this crack, you're traveling in the other direction, and you have to rotate the handle (and your hand) so you can perform the same stroke on the outside of your whip hand. The whip will be moving in a flat line parallel to the ground above your head.

Tip: make sure you're doing this on the horizontal plane. Ideally, the throws on the left and right will be mirror images of each other.

It's disconcerting at first to have the whip cracking behind you. You'll get used to it. Once you get this crack down cold, it leads quite naturally into the next crack:

**Fast Helicopter**

The Fast Helicopter is a left- and right-hand Volley on the horizontal plane above your head. It cracks at the front and back of each move on each side of you. You don't wait for the whip to follow through before you go into the corresponding crack from the other side.

Start off doing regular Helicopters, right and left, until you have a steady rhythm going. This is almost a clone of the Hassett's Four Corners.

Now you "bounce" the whip at the end of each crack and immediately reverse direction, alternating going to the inside of your wrist and going to the outside of your wrist after the whip cracks behind you.

Remember to keep your wrist pointing at the ceiling. This will help the whip stay on a flat plane as you alternate cracking on each side.

To keep the whip from hitting you in the head, angle the front crack down slightly, bringing it up as you pull it back.

Imagine standing under a sloping roof, with the roof higher behind you than it is in front of you. Follow this plane so the loop of the whip rolls back toward you above the thong leading from your hand. If it comes back under, you will whack yourself.

Be willing to contort your body, in the beginning. There's more left and right twisting to this than appears. You'll feel it in your spine. The crack feels odd, at first, because of the way the bones move against each other in your arm. It is not a natural move. With practice, it can become second nature and then give you quite an enjoyable dance with some fast, controlled cracking.

Famed whip maker Mike Murphy performed the cleanest, snappiest Helicopter I've ever seen – two-handed!

**Plane Variations**

Most of the cracks named here can be performed on other planes, and sometimes they pick up new names. Plane variations can help keep things interesting and make the best use of the space you are in. For example, as we noted above, when the Coachman's Crack is performed in the overhead plane horizontally, it gets a new name – the Helicopter.

# Chapter 8 – Two-Handed Whip Cracking

**Two-handed Timing Terms – The Train – Windshield Wipers –
Florentines – Queensland Crossovers – Parting Shots**

Being able to crack with both hands is not the same as two-handed cracking, which requires more precise timing to keep the whips from tangling up in each other.

Gary Brophy's two-handed expertise

Working with two whips will show you more than anything else that good whip work is more a matter of correct, effortless form than it is the result of muscling a whip through its arc.

Practicing two-handed routines also will wear you out a lot faster than working with one hand.

In short, two-handed whip cracking is more work, more difficult, and less forgiving than single-handed whip cracking – but when you nail it, the payoff is a tremendously good feeling.

## Two-Hand Timing Terms

These terms originated in Australia, where two-handed whip cracking is a recognized competitive sport.

**Together** means just that. You crack the whips at the same time in the same direction, your left hand mirroring your right hand.

**Staggered** means you allow one whip to lag behind the other. This gives your whips a syncopated beat.

**Balanced** means you are working the whips in opposite time to each other. For example, if you are performing Balanced

Circus Cracks, while you are coming down from the S-shape to crack one whip, the other whip is still rising. The sound of Balanced cracking is snap-pause, snap-pause, with the whips alternating in their cracking.

Each Way is when you are cracking the whips in opposite directions to each other. For example, if you are doing Each Way Circus Cracks, you are cracking forward with one hand and cracking backward with the other (a Reverse Circus Crack).

You can combine Each Way movement with the other three timing variations, so you can get Staggered Each Way, Together Each Way and balanced Each Way (which is very dramatic).

(Go too fast and you may call this Which Way timing!)

**The Train**

The Train is a two-handed Cow and Calf.

We explored the single-hand Cow and Calf in the previous chapter. If you are doing two-handed Cows and Calves, you can get a sound effect that sounds like an accelerating train.

Do the first cracks slowly in Balanced Time. This will give you an even rhythm. Now, start cracking faster.

As you pick up speed, change the timing to Staggered Time. This will sound like the clacking of the train's wheels on the rails. Go as fast as you safely can.

When you get tired (which may be in a just a few seconds), start slowing the Train down, drifting out of Staggered Time back into Balanced Time until you pull into the station and stop. Now drink a glass of lemonade.

**Windshield Wipers**

Let's start with one hand, then go to two.

Do Volleys in front of yourself, aligned with your shoulders, left to right to left. If you want to make it quicker, use the your wrist more. It's like fanning yourself with a ping pong paddle.

Once again, the key is to keep the handle almost straight. Angle the handle slightly away from you so the thong does not hit your hand on each pass.

Tip: keep the whip moving. Breaking down Volley sequences like this into bite-size pieces helps you learn the moves quicker. When you get the three-crack sequence down, go for a four-crack sequence. Then go for five.

Tip: Use your whole arm in combination with your wrist. If you use only your wrist, you will overtax your wrist muscles and irritate the carpal nerve. Using your whole arm in conjunction with the wrist gives you more control over your line and spares you from long-term problems down the road.

Aim for consistency. Each two-crack sequence should be a duplicate of the other two-crack sequences. It's when you string them together you get the long Volleys.

It is possible to crack a 6-foot whip more than 250 times in one minute. If you are cracking with both hands, double that. It's a hell of a lot of thunder in sixty seconds – and it puts you in sight of a Guinness World Record!

Remember to reach backward as well as forward. Give the whip a chance to fly. Reach!

Now use two whips. Volley left and right at the same time. One whip will always be in front of you alternating back and forth. They will not cross each other if it's done right.

It's easier to do with a stock whip, of course, because all your action can be done with your wrists (that is, the handles).

To do Windshield Wipers (or Windscreen Wipers, as it's called in Australia), you'll see that you are moving the whips in the same direction at the same time, which allows them to avoid each other.

For Irish Windshield Wipers, you move the whips in opposite directions so they're both going forward at the same time, back at the same time. The whips will cross in front of you, so a slightly Staggered Time and a slightly different angle of attack for each whip will allow you to do this without tangling.

**Florentines**

These are two-handed Overhand Flicks which cross in front of you and come back around the opposite shoulders.

Make sure you keep the whip handles straight and the planes of the whips as vertical as possible. You want the whips to crack coming down. If you make a Sidearm shot out of an Overhand Crack, you will not be lined up straight to do the follow-through to the other side.

The hand that leads, that is, the hand that goes above the other one, is called the Lead Hand.

You can add a fillip here by changing the Lead Hand, crossing one arm under the other but keeping the whip on the same side of your body. The arm on the top side will have more room to maneuver than the lower arm, so make that the arm you'll circle to come back on the underside of your other arm. To get back into regular timing, lead with this arm again to "untie" the crossed arms.

Throw your right hand forward in an Overhand Flick as you lift your left-hand whip to throw forward. As you follow through down to your left side with the right-hand whip, throw your left-hand whip forward with your left hand above your right hand. The left-hand whip will follow through on your right side and you will lift it up in a rising arc behind you as you throw the right-hand whip forward from your left side. It will follow through coming down on your right side. As it does this, throw your left-hand whip forward from your right side and use the follow through on your left side to line the left-hand whip up for the next forward throw from the left side.

I used to refer to this as "Swashbuckling," which is descriptive of the move. Two people can do this with two whips apiece for a "pirate sword fight" sequence. It's a great one to do with black lights at a sci-fi convention.

## Queensland Crossovers

With this one, we execute Slow Figure 8s on the overhand plane with both hands. It looks similar to John Brady's Under the Southern Cross. In brief, it is two-handed Helicopters.

I have also heard John Brady call it the Queensland Cross. When he visited the U.S. In 1968, he renamed it the Stars and Stripes Forever because it matched the rhythm of the patriotic song by that name.

## Parting Shots

There are many, many more cracks than these for you to discover (or create), but most will be variations on the cracks you know. For example, the Drum Roll is a two-handed Snake Killer performed in Balanced Time.

If you see some new crack that catches your breath, be assured that you can approach it, armed with the knowledge and expertise you already have.

Break a new crack down into its component parts, starting slowly then putting them together before going faster. You can add the crack later.

Some cracks are downright nasty for the level of excellence they require, like the notorious Kahona. I won't even try to describe it. One 30-second video here would be a thousand words.

## CHAPTER 9 – TRICKS AND STUNTS

**Safety – Styrofoam Strips – Popping Balloons –
Playing Cards – Snuffing Candles – Slicing Bananas –
Newspaper – Wraps & Grabs – Poker Chip Off Tongue –
Flying Streamer Cut**

**Safety – There are No Second Chances**

Tricks that can be done with a bullwhip involve cracking, targeting and wrapping. You will need to balance accuracy and safety with the dramatic effect you want.

For example, if you are cutting a cigarette from your own mouth or someone else's, understand that when the cigarette explodes it will shower flecks of tobacco and ash everywhere, possibly into the eyes of anyone standing close by. I strongly suggest you use a styrofoam strip, instead.

(If you are a professional performer, it is not a good idea to show cigarettes in the context of a show, especially if you are performing for children or their families. Relegate the cigarette cut to the tricks of yesteryear. In this age of animal-less circuses using cigarettes in a stunt dates you as a throwback to the 1940s.)

There are even safety concerns with balloons. If you put talcum powder or confetti inside a balloon so the audience can see the explosions more clearly, remember that this atomized material has to go somewhere – usually, all over the stage. This slippery material will be under the feet of the performer following you. It also will litter the stage, unless you are cleaning as you go. It breaks the feel of a show for the audience to see the artists abruptly bend over and start picking up garbage before they scamper offstage with shreds of paper in their hands.

With candles, when you crack close to melting wax, you may splash it, usually in a straight line extending through the candle to the audience or assistant in front of you.

Bear all this in mind when you are blocking out your tricks, with or without an assistant.

**Styrofoam Strips**

The best material for cutting tricks is styrofoam cut into strips from plates found in grocery store meat departments. They are light, they break easily when they are hit, and they are inexpensive (if not free).

They are also easier to see from a distance, better than sticks of spaghetti or other skinny targets. Styrofoam strips can be colored with glow-in-the-dark paint if you are doing a UV show.

Styrofoam strips are better than spaghetti for many reasons. It's easily available, easy to see and useful in a variety of contexts. And they can be cut consistently.

Gery Deer does the Throat Cut with wife Barbara. (Note: this can be dangerous.)

Dante and Mary do a double strip cut.

From a single large plate, you can cut about a dozen strips with a razor or sharp knife. Because they are brittle, I carry mine around in a round wine bottle box.

Styrofoam plates come in all colors, but go for the lighter ones (yellow, orange, white) because they are easier for the audience to see. When I carry strips in my inside vest pocket, I put them in a stiff cardboard sleeve to prevent them from breaking while I move. If you use blacklights, you can decorate the strips with florescent paint or UV markers to make them glow brightly in the dark.

Tip: You can lightly score a styrofoam strip so it breaks at a certain point (usually the middle).

Reminder: in any trick with another person, make sure you are good enough to do it before you even try. Get the trick down cold without an assistant, first. The chemistry onstage changes when you are throwing your whip in the direction of a human being. Get a good handle on the basics before you try something fancy. Push the envelope in your private practice sessions. The audience has not paid to see you screw up, so always perform slightly below your level of capability.

**Six Self-Cutting Tricks**

If you get good at this, you can slice a single strip of styrofoam a number of times before you have to reach for a fresh one. There are more than simply six ways to cut styrofoam strips you can hold for yourself, but you can experiment and create those for yourself. These are just to get you started.

The principle here is simple: visualize those railroad tracks. If the whip is traveling on a flat plane, any object that crosses that plane will be struck by the whip. If it is a strip of styrofoam, it will break.

A lot of these cuts do not rely on the popper cutting the styrofoam strip. The fall, or even the thong, may break the styrofoam. The effect is still dramatic, if you get a good crack at the end. Some folks in the audience may believe they are happening simultaneously, but even if they don't, it can still be a thrilling, effective and thrilling display of precision and daring.

**First Cut:** Hold styrofoam strip between fingers of whip hand the the strip extends out, parallel to the floor. Do a Circus Crack. As the whip passes your hand, it will strike the strip and break it. The crack follows almost immediately, adding to the effect.

**Second Cut:** Hold styrofoam strip behind your back at hip level so it extends out past your hip. When you do a Circus Crack, the popper will pass through the styrofoam strip at your side before you crack it forward.

**Third Cut:** Hold styrofoam strip behind your head at ear level so the strip extends out past your shoulder. Do a Circus Crack, and as the whip passes over your shoulder going forward, it will break the strip.

**Fourth Cut:** Stick the styrofoam through the fingers of your off hand so you can place your palm flat on your skull, the styrofoam strip sticking up like a radio antenna. Perform a Helicopter or a Cattleman's Crack above your head. The back of your hand will protect your head. Curl your fingers slightly down into your scalp to make sure. The strip will break as the whip passes through it.

**Fifth Cut:** Put your hand behind your back so the styrofoam strip extends out from under your arm, close to your body. Send the whip forward with an underhand rising crack and pull it back quickly, following through. The whip will cut the styrofom under your arm pit. The danger here is that the whip is cracking as it comes back at you. Be careful.

**Sixth Cut:** Hold the styrofoam strip with your left hand extended so it points forward about waist high. Using a longer whip, line the whip up at a 30-degree angle forward on the floor.

Use the handle and draw a short, tight circle in the air about 6 inches away from the strip. Follow through the extend your arm fully out to the side, away from your body. The whip will follow the trajectory you have drawn in the air and as it passes by the point of the circle's smallest diameter (right at the object), it will crack and slice the styrofoam strip. Wear a glove while you're practicing this one. It might not seem like it, but you will get the same forceful whack as if someone had taken deliberate aim at you from six feet away. The advantage of this particular trick is that you can do a self cut with a long whip in a tight, narrow space. I've used an 8-foot whip on a 10-foot stage for this trick.

Tip: Pay attention to the actual path of the whip. Make sure the whip connects with the strip at right angles, on the thinnest edge of its surface. This makes the cutting cleaner.

## Variations with an Assistant

**Straight Cut:** Assistant holds styrofoam strip out in hand. You cut it. Ta Daa!

**Cut from Mouth:** Assistant holds strip in mouth. The key here is to make sure the strip's thin edge is up. Make sure the strip is large enough to give you a margin for safety.

**Speed Cuts:** Assistant holds styrofoam strips between fingers in both hands and angles them to be cut one at a time with consecutive cracks.

**Three Strips at once:** Assistant holds styrofoam strips parallel to each other in mouth and both hands, all three above each other so that one Circus Crack will break all three.

**Two-Handed Strip Cutting:** Using a behind-the-back switch, the whip handler cracks consecutive strips held alternately in the left and right hands of the assistant. Go through six or eight strips.

**Contortionist Cuts:** Assistant vamps with styrofoam strips by hitting sexy, tensed poses which allow the whip cracker to target the strips from different angles.

## Popping Balloons

Balloons can be problematic. Avoid balloons advertised as being good for helium. This latex is thicker, dense, harder to pop. Water-bomb balloons can be pop resistant, even though are supposedly made to break. These balloons are intended to explode at the slightest touch, but that has not been my experience.

The key is to inflate a balloon to the point of bursting. If the skin of the balloon is slightly soft, it will absorb the blow from the whip's popper and not explode. If you hit it with the knot in the popper, you have to really whack it. Point and Squeeze to crack the whip just as the popper touches the

Chapter 9 - Tricks & Stunts    || 85

balloon. If the whip cracks before you hit the balloon, you will merely wallop the balloon and not pop it.

I have tried various cutting cheats. I had some limited success with a bit of paper clip twined into the popper like a twist of barbed wire. The knot helped keep the paper clip from flying off into the audience after hitting the target, but this was no guarantee. In the interests of safety, I discontinued the practice. It also limited the use of the whip to that single trick, since I didn't want to be doing wraps, say, with a whip that could cut like a Russian knout if my aim was off.

The addition of a gimmick like this also impeded the smooth flow of the popper and made a crack less likely to achieve consistently.


**Playing Cards**

Playing cards are not all the same. Bicycle playing cards and other cards which are coated with plastic slice cleanly. Simple pasteboard cards may slice, maybe not. A playing card is about as small as you can get with a hand-held object which can still be seen by the people in the balcony seats.

Have the assistant show the card to the audience, white side out. Let the audience see the pips on the card. This makes it real.

Assistant holds the card in her right hand, looking over her right shoulder at you. The advantage of this position for all holding tricks is that the arm acts like a shield for the front of the body and face, should the air conditioning come on and the breeze blow the whip in her direction (it's happened to me).

The card needs to be held at the upper corner horizontally, with the short side butted against the fingers of the same hand. This is to create a firm, unyielding edge. Otherwise, you may cut halfway through the card and send the remnant flying out of your holder's hand. Not classy.

The whip cracker cannot see behind the card, so her thumb gripping the back of the card should not extend past her finger on the front of the card. If you make sure you are not hitting her finger, you can assume it's not going to hit her thumb, either.

It helps if the assistant holds the card with the white side toward you. This makes the card easier to target in the varying light of different venues.

Crack outside for distance and move in toward the card. You should get to the point that you can

Dante and Mary cut the cards

predictably get to the edge of the card in one or two cracks before you cut it. And it builds the suspense.

Don't target the middle of the card. Remember that the holder's hand is taking up a portion of the card, so what looks like the center of the card is actually closer to the fingers than the real center line of your target.

After the card is cut, your assistant should hold the card up with the white side toward the

audience. They can clearly see there is a slice missing from the card, pips missing. If the assistant holds the card up with the back side to the audience, the mosaic style of the back of the card will make seeing the trick's success more difficult to see immediately.

If the cut piece falls at her feet, it is appropriate to pick both pieces up to show the audience, one piece in each hand. This dramatizes the actual slice.

Understand that when the audience applauds, it is not only clapping for your expertise. It is honoring the amazing bravery of your assistant as well. Acknowledge your assistant. The audience will love you all the more for it. She deserves this accolade, since it takes both of you to make these tricks work.

For another trick, I sometimes pull the playing card out of my own pocket and show it to the audience. I walk over to my assistant and place the card not in her hand, but between her teeth. As I turn my back, the assistant plays with the audience's fears by staring wide-eyed at the card under her nose, then shaking her head emphatically and taking the card out of her mouth to hold it in her hand – which is how we'd planned to do the trick in the first place. This heightens the anxiety of the audience and then gives them a moment of comedy relief before the dangerous work resumes for real.

The great Vince Bruce showed that it is possible to cut cards as they are flipped through the air. I used to do this until I saw that a card could be hit in such a way that it could fly into the audience. And as some sideshow performers have demonstrated, ordinary playing cards can be flipped so they spin quickly can cut targets as surely as knives. I discontinued these stunts in my shows, but I still like the challenge in my private practices.

Use the right cards. I recommend Bicycle playing cards. They are exactly alike (for your purpose), and they have a light coat of plastic which makes them slice superbly. Also, use a shorter whip. The shorter the whip, the easier it will be.

The key to this trick is to crack consistently at the same imaginary spot in the air, and then to throw the playing cards consistently into the same spot. Tine it so they meet each other at the same moment.

To get this stunt down, practice throwing the cards without a whip. Use what's called a Magician's Flip, which is a flat toss with a spin so the card pauses in the air as it spins. Do this by putting an index finger along the long side of the card. Cock your wrist as you draw your arm back. As you do a backhand throw with a card, uncock your wrist so you make the card spin as much as you can without making it sail across the room. You want it to hang in the air at a predictable point in front of you.

Practice until you can toss the card with your left hand and crack the whip with your right hand so they cross that imaginary point in front of you at the same speed, every time. When you get this part down, add the whip in your right hand. (I've found a Staggered Timing works best.)

Begin with circus cracks, over and over, cracking the whip at exactly the same point in the air in front of you. When you are consistent, we can start to put these two elements of this stunt together.

Continue cracking, moving your other hand to throw those imaginary cards into the spot where the crack occurs. It's all timing. Let it get into your body via muscle memory. That's what you're after, knowing how long it takes the whip to crack, how long it takes for that card to reach that same point, and how much of a lag between the two you need. When you can time it so the card meets the whip, you'll start knocking the cards out of the air. Here, you'll see you may not be able to predict where the card will go when it's hit.

Remember that you're not trying to knock the card out of the air with the whip, you are throwing the card into the whip's crack. It is a visualization that helped me.

Now stick an open box of cards into your belt on your throwing hand's side. You can pull the cards one at a time out of the box until you have gone through the whole deck. This is much easier than trying to hold a lot of cards in your hand and throw them individually.

Play a "personal best" game. See how many of the cards you can hit per deck, and what percentage of those are cut. With practice, they'll both improve.

In an ideal universe, with enough practice you could hypothetically make your whip aim and card toss coincide consistently enough that you could do this trick blindfolded.

For obvious reasons, this is an indoor trick.

**Candle Snuffing**

Set the candle chest-high on a stable surface. Secure the candle holder (tape it down).

Otherwise, if you touch the candlestick you will you may knock it over and send a waterfall of wax cascading to the floor.

Make sure the wick is high enough to light. If you've used the candle for this before, you may have knocked the wick down to a nub.

Tip: With each individual crack, you will create three chances to snuff the candle.

If you snuff a candle with an Overhand Flick, aim slightly above the flame. At the end of the throw, hold your hand still so the crack occurs right above the flame.

Here's the cheat: First, the candle may be snuffed by the breeze you create in throwing the whip toward the wick. Second, the actual crack can create a wave that puffs the candle out without touching it (this is a clean snuff which is your goal). Third (worst case scenario), after the crack the popper can come back and just stroke the top of the wick, extinguishing the flame. You'll need to be precise or you'll be showering candle wax all over the place. It's easier to do it right. If you are using Circus Crack, aim slightly below the flame.

The size of the candle has nothing to do with the trick. This works with huge cathedral candles and tiny birthday candles alike. I have used it with tiki torches.

Tip: If you use an assistant to hold the candle, make sure she is not standing behind the candle, in a line from you to the candle to her. You may shower her with hot wax. Have her face the audience and hold the candle in front of her, standing at right angles to you. Or have her hold the candle out to her side as she faces you directly.

**Slicing a Banana**

Have your holder grip the banana (or zucchini or cucumber) tightly, or it will go flying when it is hit. The banana needs to be held solidly. If it moves even slightly after it is hit, it will absorb the blow and not slice. The grip should be a tight clasp, with a firm hand anchoring the banana.

Otherwise, the hand itself will act like a shock absorber. If the banana is dangled nervously by the fingertips, it will be knocked to the floor.

If the assistant is skittish, allow padded gloves to be worn. Once they see you can do the stunt without touching their fingers, they will be more confident about holding for you. In short, perform below your level of capability. Never, in a show, should you make a throw thinking, "I wonder if I can make this one work." Practice on your own time, not your assistant's.

A shorter whip will be more accurate because you are standing closer to your target (ie use a 6-foot whip instead of a 12-foot whip).

Use a firm banana. A soft banana will just split or explode. You want a clean, knife-like slice. If it is soft, the blow will merely puree the contents of the banana skin. It will act as a shock absorber. A cooler banana (not frozen) cuts more easily than a warm one.

Aim for the end of the banana. Give your assistant a margin for safety. Have her angle the banana slightly so it is parallel to the floor, giving you a longer target to aim for with a vertical stroke.

Make sure your stroke does not cross the plane of the assistant's body (Inside the Tracks/Outside the Tracks) – it doesn't look good to hit her in the knees after you slice the banana.

Use a thinner (sharper) popper about 6 inches long.

Hit the banana with either a Circus Crack or an Overhand Flick, and add a squeezed-handle grace note to supercharge the crack.

Try to lay the popper in so the banana is hit across the middle of the popper and does not touch the fall. If the banana is hit by the fall or any other part of the whip, it will not slice. It will explode and splatter as surely as if Gallagher had hit it with a sledge hammer. If it's a good night and I'm on my game, I can take slices off the banana two or three inches at time.

This is a morbidly funny trick for an adult audience because of the phallic overtones. If your assistant holds the banana at groin level, you will see out of the corner of your eye grown men jerk their knees together when the banana is cut.

Build the tension by doing slow and sensual wraps on the banana, first. This way, the moment of the slicing stroke will come as a greater shock.

Make sure the stage manager knows to clean the stage afterward, especially if you are followed by dancers. The remains of the banana are slippery and could be a danger for the footing of performers who follow you. The joke of someone slipping on a banana peel is not funny when it is another performer being messed up because you were not taking care of the consequences of your own act. Be considerate and responsible. If you're in a show, you're part of a team.

## Cutting Newspapers

A good newspaper cut starts before you even throw the whip. Pick your newspaper carefully.

Experiment with it. A typical newspaper has some sheets printed on thinner or thicker pages than the other pages. Color pages (grocery ads) tend to be thicker sheets, which are harder to cut.

Further, the newspaper will have a grain, so it will tear straight in one direction but skew off if you cut across the grain. Have your assistant hold the paper with the grain running straight up and down for the first cut.

Here's the procedure: Your assistant faces you with the newspaper held tightly at the top corners, pulling slightly to make the upper edge of the paper taut. If the top edge is not tight, you will crumple the paper when you want it to slice. Keep the tautness all the way through the crack or the slice will lose its power midway through the paper.

Gary Brophy bravely holds newspaper for his daughter Jacinta.

I sometimes play with this by being blindfolded and having my assistant tear the paper as though I have cut it, even though I am missing it by a good foot (deliberately). The audience and the assistant are now in on the joke together. The audience laughs when I remove the blindfold to see how well I've done, and take my big bow.

But this is comedy. Here's how to do the stunt for real, I suggest this: The assistant's arms should be fully extended, holding the newspaper as far away from her body as possible. As each crack slices the newspaper down the middle, some assistants crumple one half of the used sheet in one hand (or simply drop it) and hold the remaining paper in the same spot in space. This is so the whip cracker does not have to aim afresh every time.

Each new (smaller) rectangle of newspaper should be held at the upper two corners to create a firm, tight edge for the whip's popper (not the fall) to slice through. Once the newspaper gets down to a smallish size, you can cut across the grin with impunity. Hold the newspaper so the longest edge is always horizontal, giving a bigger target to the whip cracker. The possibility of a partial cut diminishes with each successive cut, since the pieces are getting smaller and the whip's popper has more chance to travel through the whole scrap.

When the page has been sliced three or four times (or when the assistant gets nervous), the holder can now turn slightly to present what's left of the newspaper with a single hand. The trick here is to hold the fragment at precisely the same point in space where the full newspaper was. The whip handler does not need to take aim from scratch, just be consistent.

A Circus Crack works best to start this one. Bring the whip down on a specific line. To keep from hitting the paper on the upstroke, rock back a few inches and shorten the arm extension. Go full distance on the down stroke.

The rhythm of this trick is important. Getting started, use one crack for distance, one crack to cut, one crack for distance, one crack to cut. Bang-bang-Bang-Bang for two cuts. The "distance crack" is the pause your assistant needs to position the paper for the next cutting crack. Some acts can do this with a cut every crack.

It's your choice about how small to make that last piece of paper. Some folks like to get it down to a business card size, some folks shoot for postage stamp size. You can keep going until the last cut disappears from the assistant's fingers (because she lets go), in which case she should smile triumphantly and show her empty hand to the audience to prove she still has all her fingers.

Slicing a newspaper off a person's back without nicking them is an edgy trick. It should probably be one of the last stunts in your show.

Here's the how-to: Prepare the newspaper ahead of time by putting duct tape along the short sides of the newspaper. Overlap it, so half of the tape extends beyond the paper.

When the moment comes for this trick, have your brave assistant remove her top or coat or otherwise bare her back (no, nudity is not required). Take the prepared newspaper page and attach one strip at the top of her back between the shoulder blades so the newspaper hangs loosely

Robert Dante and the Daring Tina finish up on the right foot.

down her back.

Have the assistant stretch her hands out to her sides, lightly forward. She should now push her tummy forward and her butt backward. Attach the bottom of the newspaper to the buttocks so you make a large gap between the newspaper and her skin.

If you look at your assistant in profile, you will see that because of her posture, the newspaper is stretched taut but her body is curled serpentine fashion. She should look like a capital letter D. There should be a sizable hollow space between the paper and her back. This is her safety margin.

Using sidearm shots sent out parallel to the ground, start cracking the whip outside the newspaper, following through on a flat trajectory until you touch the paper. Be prepared to shift slightly to the left or right to get the right angle. She should not move at all.

Sono Osato whirled her whip and flipped her dress like a matador's cape in "The Kissing Bandit."

You should just brush the outside edge of the newspaper and nick it without touching her back. Once an initial cut is started, you can continue to to tear the paper by touching the edge of the rip in the paper. After three or four of these, the paper will fall apart into two pieces.

The hardest part of this stunt is to get that first cut started.

It is vital to this trick that you know your distance. Practice with the same whip you'll be using in performance. Practice with the same length of popper. Make sure your assistant understands how important it is to not move forward or backward, which would change the depth of the safety margin.

She should maintain the same position throughout the trick. If she shrugs to adjust her position, the tape could come loose and allow the newspaper to actually lie flat against her back. There will be no margin for safety. When the trick is performed correctly, the newspaper catches all the strokes. It is not necessary for your assistant to be a masochist – just a brave person. But you'd better be spot on for this.

### Wraps and Grabs

To snatch and grab something from someone's hand (like a knife or a sword), do a gentle wrap. Lock the fall with a flip and pull taut. You'll get to the point where you can do the crack and grab simultaneously. Watch your face! The object you grab will come sailing back at you – be prepared to catch it. I've used a realistic looking plastic knife, and it would not do to skewer myself before the

end of the performance. If you strike with
you will slap the target hard and probably
firmly. You can still get a loud crack, but it
more accurate, as well.

I particularly love t        is    ith scarves a
much. The   ip     t  av   much chance
scarf wraps  ro       fall and follows it, s
will fly off    whip back into the air. Whe
the air.

### Bullwhip Tango

This is a choreographed dance consisting
The wraps are executed with Circus Cracks
Assistants should be prepared to spin out t
Wraps include double self wraps (good clo
simultaneously, bear in mind that spinning
once with two whips are hard to spin out o

                  e side
                  es and
                  an faci

                  o's fil
                  t's all a

                  on You
                  Kissing Bandit.

Explorer Hiram Bingham (left) was the real-life model for the character of Indiana Jones.

Born Nov. 19, 1875, Bingham was not a professional archeologist., but he was one of the first to recognize the

urs or the   fo   hard  . Leave it for the professionals. Bingham
mply said, "Don't do it!"  guides to find the Incan mountain fortress of Machu Picchu in 1911. His lectures introduced the world to this rediscovery.

ue to read.
He was an avid aviator and academic, teaching politics and
ngue. She angles the blade backward so it does not have a tongue of
ward are to miss her nose. Using the point and squeeze ham
                 died in 1956 and is interred at Arlington National Cemetery.
oudly to terrify the audience, then cracked gingerly as a

> The Indiana Jones movies have done more to popularize bullwhips than any other cultural phenomenon in the United States.
>
> Colin Wilby (right) demonstrates the attention to detail that marks a top-notch cos-player, right down to the Mark VII gas mask bag and the David Morgan bullwhip with a wrist loop.

delicate wrap so that only the gentle momentum of the fall actually takes the coin or poker chip off the tongue.

Note: This can be seen on videos by the great Australian whip cracker John Brady and his wife Vi. A classic!

**Flying Streamer Cut**

Tie a weight to the end of a piece of string, then attach a crepe streamer to the weight.
The assistant swings the string with the streamer in a big circle (using the whole arm so there's a safety margin) just enough to keep the string taut. As she swings the streamer, the whip handler cracks and cuts pieces off the end of the streamer, again and again.

The trick, of course, is the timing. Lifting the whip and bringing it down at a specific point usually takes the same amount of time each time. You'll want to figure out where the streamer should be in relation to your assistant when you start the crack. As the streamer is cut, it becomes lighter which can make the speed of the swing increase. You'll need to adjust your start point accordingly for each crack.

The streamer can be swung vertically or horizontally, or even diagonally. Cuts can be achieved with Circus Cracks or Overhand Flicks (remember to allow for the differing depths of these cracks).

The end of the trick is signified by the assistant when she lets the streamer (or what's left of it) ground out before she raises her arms triumphantly to the audience.

Gary Brophy and daughter Jacinta perform a streamer cutting stunt for a circus audience.

I practice this using poi, attaching the crepe streamer with duck tape. I can stretch the duration of this otherwise brief stunt if I target the tail's last couple of inches. Make sure the depth is precise – if you hit it with the fall instead of the cracker, you'll rip instead of cutting, and you may yank a large section of the streamer off the string. Remember that the whip follows through after the crack, so make sure your partner is in the Safe Zone.

# CHAPTER 10 - PERFORMING

*Be Professional – Create a Character – Choreography –
Rehearsing – Using Black Lights – Dress the Part (Costumes) –
Assistants – Venues – Handling Tangled Lashes –
Dancing on the Edge*

**Be Professional**

I receive a call recently, asking me if I would appear at a charity benefit function. I agreed (this isn't always about money), and I asked about the specifics for our show.

What's the date and time? How long do we perform? What's the space like? Who's the audience? What's the lighting? Is there a sound system? Do I tell stories or do I work mute? Do we supply our own music, or is there a DJ?

If this had been a paying gig, we would have talked about money. We would have discussed a contract or a letter of agreement. (I also request a non-refundable deposit. A handshake agreement used to be enough – Not any more.)

Let's say someone asks you to crack your whip at their event, or fundraiser, or party. How do you do this in such a way that it is entertaining, safe and enjoyable for everyone (including you)?

The answer is to be a professional about it. This means your work begins before you step onstage.

**Create a Character**

Simply executing tricks is not performing. I have seen many technically excellent but lifeless and limp whip performances. Expensive costumes by themselves are not enough to compensate for a listless presentation.

Give yourself a character to be when you perform. It can be almost anything. There are vampire whip crackers, cosmic cowgirls, clowns, gunslingers, Celts in kilts.

The character should be an extension or exaggeration of yourself so you never have to worry about breaking character.

Most performing experts agree this is the most important question to ask yourself: "What is my character?" As Andrew Conway so succinctly puts it, "An act begins with the character, not the tricks."

He's right!

Ask yourself, "Who am I performing?" Even Nietzsche noted that where people might see "a great man," he usually saw an ordinary man acting out his own ideal image of himself. Do it consciously and you can claim the power to be great!

Joyce Rice was a national Champion baton twirler when she was a youngster, so it was natural for her to prefer to use shorter whips and to incorporate flips, twirls and twists into her routines. Her appearances were bright, bouncy, giddy, and gleeful affairs.

I am relatively lucky in this department. I perform my Self – but over the top.

My personna is arrogant, pompous, "Eat up with myself," as Southerners would say. I act like I think I am the bee's knees. This way, when my assistant pops my self-delusional balloon and brings me back down to earth, it's a satisfying experience for everyone. It's a Punch and Judy Show. We all like to see the villain get his comeuppance. The key here is to be abashed and amused, to laugh at myself. This takes the cruelty out of it and makes it a morality play. It humanizes my assistant, too, when she twits me like a Tinkerbell on behalf of the audience. And it allows folks to look past the monstrous cardboard-front ego to see the very real skill and professionalism at work by both of us. By the end of the show, they can see quite clearly that we are truly a Team-- and that we had Great Fun getting there.


## Choreography

No one does it the same way, so all I can do here is to tell you how I do it. Perhaps it will help you. At the worst, it gives you another perspective.

I've got the gig. Now I must ask myself questions. How long do I have? Is the space bullwhip-friendly or do I have to make adjustment in the act? What's the audience going to be like? Is it a mute show or do I use patter as I perform? Who handles the lights? Do I supply music or do they?

I know what tricks I can perform safely, and I have a repertoire of stories with which to regale my listeners. Now, I get out my stopwatch, a pencil, and a pad of paper.

Let's say, hypothetically, I have 5 minutes, no patter, straight circus performance or nightclub variety act. I break the 5 minutes into segments. I'll take 30 seconds and do a solo whip routine, starting with a single whip and then going into a two-handed routine. Even though I've already warmed up backstage, I use the easy stuff to get me into my groove. While I'm doing this, my assistant sets up the props (ie candles, styrofoam strips) on the other side of the stage. She should be quick and inconspicuous so she doesn't draw attention away from you. It's a trade-off, so she should minimize her non-performing activity. She will have her chance to shine shortly!

At the end of the routine, I give the audience opportunities to express itself, by a pause, a smile, a pose. A fast volley routine which stops with a couple of loud cracks will get applause in the middle of a show and at the end. (Thank you, Andrew, for the suggestion!)

Even if I've screwed up (no one's perfect), there's always enough worth applauding. It's entertainment, not the Olympics!

If you screw up, don't pretend you didn't. The audience saw it, so play with it. Try again, with a shrug and a big smile, or a joke. This keeps the audience from being embarrassed for you, and it shows you are still in control of the performance. This is vital for the audience to have confidence in you, to maintain belief.

If my aim is slightly off and I have cracked several times without hitting the target held by my assistant, I may pause, scratch my head, squint as though I am trying to see where the light is, then I walk forward, take my assistant's shoulders in my hands and move her three inches to the left. I walk back to my spot and sight down the whip, pretending it was all her fault for not being in the right place. By this time, the spell is broken, and the cut usually follows precisely. And the audience thinks it is part of the act.

I had the good fortune years ago to see Vladimir Horowitz perform a piano concert. He did this: He sat down, began to play, stopped immediately and walked offstage. Two stage hands hurried out with a tape a tape measure and measured the distance between the piano and the bench. They moved the bench – I swear it's true! - two inches further away from the piano. They hustled into the wings. Horowitz walked back out, took another bow, sat down, and played the most eloquent music I'd heard in years, faultlessly.

Back to the bullwhips: Three is a good number of times to try to nail a trick. The second try raises the tension level, which is relieved when it is successfully executed on the third try. If you can't do it on the third try, substitute something simpler and add a bit of flash to it. Then move on.

Sometimes the knots on your whips will tangle. This is why you really should have backup whips with you. Go with the flow, keep it moving. You're on a schedule, and you can't lose the audience for a moment!

Keeping all this in mind, I've still got a little more than 4 minutes to fill. Cutting a newspaper, popping balloons, cutting a playing card, snuffing a candle may take 3 minutes.

At this point, I can take one minute to indulge in a sensual tango-style dance with my partner, doing wraps and grabs, allowing her to draw attention to herself and her bravery. At the end of this section, we bow – both of us. Because it literally takes two to tango.

Not every show is put together the same way as the others. You must grab the audience first, and your second-best trick is a good way to start. Your best trick should be your closer, leaving the audience wanting more. And you may be surprised to hear that your best trick may not be the hardest trick. Judge by the audience's satisfaction, the "Wow!" Factor.

Since it's a mute show, I need music. You can find buy-out music, royalty-free music, or Creative Commons music from many places on the internet. Yes, your use of a popular cover by a band might be covered by the club's license, but don't assume, because infringing someone's copyright will come back to bite you in the ass somewhere down the road.

If you buy the music on a CD, the sections are usually broken down by different lengths. The nice thing about this sort of "canned music" is that the sections usually dovetail into each other seamlessly, allowing me to create the music that suits my style. I rehearse to the music so I will be able to keep track of where I am in my performance by recognizing specific musical markers. I like driving, dramatic melodies, and sinuous bellydance/fusion music. I prefer to not use music with lyrics (yes, Louis Prima's "Enjoy Yourself" would be an exception if I could get the rights).

Equally important is to make sure everything works together. If my show is at a Western venue, I don't wear my tails and play Goth music. Dress appropriately. Give the audience every reason to love you!

You can't cram all you know into 5 minutes. Don't even try. For example, I may want to highlight a specific routine, like a blindfold sequence, but I'll use some of the other stunts to build up to that.

A note on the blindfold: Yes, you can use a trick blindfold that you can see through, but if you'd rather do the real thing, here's how: assistant holds target a few feet away from the proposed arc of the whip. You do a "distance crack." If you are consistent, she knows this is where the next crack will come. For added effect, she may say, "Left three inches!" You must ignore her and crack at exactly the same spot as before, but now she knows where to hold the target so you'll hit it.

I've had the best fortune working with dancers, especially belly dancers, as assistants. I enjoyed the luxury of working with Tina Ritt, who also cracks whips credibly. As a professional belly dancer, she knew how to move, so that when she cracked the whip, it became a mesmerizing moment that I could not achieve myself. This talent of knowing where to be, and when, precisely, expanded the possibilities tremendously. It made her an important partner in the act. Especially because if she wasn't where she was supposed to be, I was the one who looked bad.

**Rehearsing**

Rehearse the individual elements of the performance, then practice how they go together. Do not assume a thing (bullwhips are dangerous enough by themselves , so stack all the odds in your favor). With my assistant, I even practice walking onstage. Practice your bows. Practice in costume a few times. When I do a full-on dress rehearsal, I practice everything from the dressing room to the stage and back. This might be a bit much for others, but when I walk out there I do not want to have one moment of self-doubt, or to wander what's next.

Visualize the whole routine in your mind! Drill it in so deep you can do it without thinking, or even while you're talking about something else. You'll be glad you took the bit of extra time to do it.

It is important to rehearse to the music. I like to use the music to tell me which stunt comes next, and how long I have to go before the next trick.

I sometimes use silent signals with my assistant. I do not want to be shouting or waving my arms like a traffic cop. You can work out your own, but are two I've used: if I touch my nose, it means she's too close to me and she needs to back away a bit. If I reach across my body to touch my wrist, it means I need her to move closer. She will now be able to make her final adjustment in relation to the sound of the whip cracking off to her side in my "distance crack" setup.

It helps to make any signals intuitive, natural. The "move back" signal of touching/holding my nose is the same as saying "I don't like the smell of this." Holding an arm across my body so I'm almost embracing myself means "I need a hug," which means I want her to move closer to me.

Please don't read more into this than I intend. A professional doesn't mix Church and State – your assistant is your working partner, not your love bunny.

## Using Black Lights

Find a good whip maker who works with nylon or paracord. Run samples under a hand-held black light to see how it glows. Get your whips made of this material.

I got a pair of neon yellow cow whips from Rhett Kelly. Working with them was laborious because of the clunky handles. I removed them and out the thongs on ordinary stock whip handles, and the whips worked beautifully. I could now do the cutting tricks and the two-handed routines I desired.

Chris Camp dresses the part in an outfit that is as functional as it is eye-catching

I would say the art has progressed far enough that well made nylon whips can be on a par with kangaroo whips, and at a fraction of the cost. It's your choice.

The bright yellow of my whips' thongs glowed electrically under the black lights. Flourescent-style black lights take about 120 flashes a second which results in whips leaving "trails" in the air, the stroboscopic memory of the whip's movement. This can be distracting when you're working, so you need to be sure you can crack the whips with your eyes closed. You'll rely more on feel than sight under black light, because when you see the whip it will have already gone past that point.

You can add black light makeup, hair spray, phosphorescent clothing. If you don't, the whips will look like they're floating in space (great for a "Sorcerer's Apprentice" routine!). My assistant holds styrofoam strips which have been sprayed with glow-in-the-dark paint. The same spray paint can be used on other props.

Black lights only work if the audience sees the object bathed in the IV light. If anything comes between the black light and your props, the shadow will make the prop stop glowing. It helps to have black lights aimed at you from two angles. The room should be as dark as possible to maximize the black light. Even a little white light or daylight can ruin the effect.

Florescent paint and Glo-tape actually shine brighter the longer they are exposed to black light.

Try to keep your whips off the floor. Dirty whips lose their sharp black light effect. Store them in plastic bags or pillow cases. When you travel with them, keep them apart from your leather whips so the leather conditioner in your 'roo whips won't rub off onto them.

**Dress the Part (Costumes)**

**Wear suspenders or a dance belt!** You're going to be moving vigorously, and a belt won't do the job. I knew a juggler who safety-pinned his shirt to the inside of his pants so it wouldn't work itself up while he juggled.

Jasmine Jackdaw takes aim on 'The Rumbucket.'

Dress for the venue. Cowboy clothes for rodeo, vampire formal for Goth clubs, whatever is appropriate.

Practice in costume! Some spinning moves may not work with tux tails or long dresses. High heels or clunky boots may look great on your assistant but they are no good if they put her off balance. One wrap at a moment of imbalance and she may tumble to the floor.

Keep your costumes clean and pressed. You're a professional, so dress like it. Look like you just came out of the plastic wrapper. Your hosts don't want someone in jeans and sneakers. They want to feel like they're getting their money's worth.

Avoid costumes that restrict movement. If gloves are worn, make them as skin-tight as you can so your dexterity is not compromised. Avoid danglies and bangles, necklaces, fringes, and other things that can hang off a costume. I guarantee your whip will catch these, and always at the worst moment. If you still want these in your performance, practice to see where problems might arise and adjust the act accordingly.

When you travel, take a few choices of costumes. It doesn't help to dress all in black, just to see the curtain behind you is all-black, as well. You will look like a floating head as your costume disappears into the background!

Look at other performers' costumes, from all genres, from ice skaters to movie characters. They can give you some good ideas.

## Assistants

What does it take to be a Bullwhip Assistant? More than you might think, because a good bullwhip act is made up of everyone doing a good job in front of the audience.

There are great solo acts (Vince Bruce and Joyce Rice leap to mind), and there are performers who use volunteers from the audience effectively (and safely).

If you are using a holder, understand that they do not simply hold and pose. She (or he) is as important to the success of a performance as the supposed star is. In reality, you are both stars.

## Intelligence

In my experience, a good Target Girl/Boy knows as much about bullwhips as you do. They may know how to crack, as well., which will give an added dimension to your presentation.

They can anticipate what is going to happen onstage and can adapt their movements to fit the limitations of the venue (ie Where are the lights? Can the audience see everything? Is the area safe for performing sometimes risky maneuvers?)

They'll be smart enough to understand acceptable risks, and will approach dangerous stunts with caution. They guarantee the odds are stacked in their favor. They don't take unneeded risks. Being brave does not mean being stupid (even though courage is definite prerequisite!). And, it goes without saying, they do not perform drunk, stoned or otherwise incapacitated.

## Look for a Dancer

The great whip cracker Brian Chic told me he found his best assistants at dance studios. This been my experience, too. They don't need to be professional — just good.

A good dancer knows how to move gracefully (and in an adult show, sensuously). SThey have impeccable timing, since they are moving with the whips. It helps if they also have good comedic timing so they can play with the audience. They know how to dance with their partner, the whip cracker. A top-notch bullwhip performance is a duet, so they must be an active partner, not a passive one. They can't stand there like a mannequin or the audience will fall asleep, no matter how good the whip cracker is!

Dante and Mary segue from newspaper and styrofoam strip cutting into the start of a Wrap Dance onstage.

The assistant "sells" the tricks to the audience. They help to set up the routines and then help the audience appreciate what happened. They are the divine (or impish) intermediary between the whip cracker and the audience. They are their guide, the one who makes human contact with audience members. Few viewers will be able to relate to the whip cracker, especially if he is that good, but they can certainly empathize with the assistant who may be in danger. The audience fears for the passive partner, they have concern for their safety. It is the Perils of Pauline, and the audience rejoices when the assistant escapes unharmed. When that happens, they appreciate the assistant's courage much more than the whip cracker's skill.

In performance or rehearsal, one should be in the moment, present and alert, so I'll repeat the warning made above: Alcohol or drugs will throw timing and dexterity off, and that's when accidents happen.

As politically incorrect as it may be, a sexy female assistant can add "eye candy" to a show, and this can work to the whip handler's advantage.

A magician's assistant traditionally dresses in skimpy or revealing clothing to distract the audience. With a bullwhip artist, this is not only because it titillates the audience but because this beauty and vulnerability make stunts seem more dangerous, so the payoff is more satisfying when she escapes harm. She distracts the audience from mundane stage business which may occur in a show. She also emphasizes the erotic aura that surrounds daredevils. Fear is arousing, and people want to be thrilled and entertained.

**Professional attitude**

Bullwhip performing is an art and a skill, but it is show business as much as it's a display of technical accuracy. The first job of a bullwhip team is to entertain – the whip is merely the vehicle by which this is accomplished. This is supported by using costumes, lights, music, choreography, well written scripts and well executed performances – which are the result of rehearsals, rehearsals, rehearsals.

A bullwhip act is a romantic adventure with intangible rewards which can be tremendously satisfying. Unfortunately, it's not likely you will get rich doing this, but you may be able to make a decent income. Many good performers use whips as an adjunct to other skills like trick roping, juggling, knife throwing, magic, trick riding or stunt work. In my own life, I have found that private lessons, group demos and sales of whip-related products account for a good portion of my performing income.

Professional athletes put their uniforms on and show up, even if they don't feel like being in the stadium that day. The good ones are on time, and they deliver what they are paid to provide.

When they do their jobs right, come to see them again. They are constantly trying to raise their level of excellence. The good ones do not believe their own propaganda. They know they are only as good as their last game, so the top pros are the ones who get out there and practice, practice, practice. They may love the game, but they also know they have to work to stay at the top of their game.

**Balancing reality and artistry**

Don't have any illusions – you'll never be as good as you want to be. You may also be criticized for things outside your control. If something can screw up a performance, at some point it will, and in ways you could not anticipate. You can't let yourself get away with a thing, because the audience certainly won't. And the act has to come first, so you must be willing to make sacrifices (yes, on a weekend you might want to get away to the beach, but a performance set for a Saturday night cannot be rescheduled.).

Ideally, an assistant brings passion and creativity to the act as much as the whip handler. It does help to watch other disciplines, and if you see something that will enhance your whip act, go for it.

There may be days when you might think that no activity is worth such effort and inconvenience. But then there comes that moment when you see a facial expression on someone watching you that makes you realize the experience is surpassing your wildest dreams.

And that you are having FUN.
No bullwhip artist – or magician – can do everything alone. The assistant is as important to the success of a performance as the whip cracker is.

Naomi Damian combines dance moves with LED whips in her visually stunning nightclub act.

## Venues

Most bullwhip acts perform at rodeos and Wild West shows for family-oriented audiences. But there are other venues, including circuses, county fairs, art fairs, cruise ships, corporate events, theme parks, private parties, stage plays, films, schools, libraries, and adult-oriented events.

I've performed at charity events and fetish fashion shows, with only slight changes necessary to make the presentation suit the different audiences.

In this area, it really is a case of "It's not what you do, it's the way that you do it."

**Handling Tangled Lashes**

A young friend in Ohio wrote to me about a show he did. Sure enough, the nightmare of all professional bullwhip artists happened to him – he knotted his popper and fall.

Fortunately, he had the presence of mind to relate a funny story while he made his quick repair, and he was able to resume the show without losing his audience.

There are things you can do to minimize this pitfall.

1. Don't condition your whip less than 24 hours before a show. The conditioner can make the fall "tacky" so it wants to grab your popper.

2. Have a backup whip you can grab quickly. Ideally, it is identical to the first whip, a matched pair.

3. Make your popper shorter. Longer poppers are more likely to tangle. Practice cutting with shorter poppers, because the depth will be different from long poppers.

4. Learn the trick of "setting your whip," or "grounding" it, during a show. It makes your shots straighter, less loopy. And it can add a flair to your presentation if you do it with style, fluidly.

5. Get a couple of comedy shticks you can use if the whip does tangle. It's okay if you crash and burn, as long as it's entertaining and no one gets hurt. The truth is that the venue is not paying you to be an excellent whip handler. They are paying you to entertain the audience. And just as you'll never find a juggler who never dropped a ball, you will probably never meet a whip handler who doesn't have some story about a tangled whip, or the like.

If you enjoy traveling, if you are an exhibitionist, if you like people (and like to meet people), if you want to do something few people have done, if you'd like to create memories for a lifetime, if you want to stand out from the crowd, if this sort of life sounds exciting to you, then this is your invitation to the dance. Start where you are. Get cracking!

# CHAPTER II – TEACHING OTHERS

## Safety First – Teaching Tips

**Safety First**

Have extra safety glasses on hand if other people are cracking, and make sure they actually use them.
Make sure everyone reads the safety rules and signs off on them. I suggest that no more than one person cracks at a time. If there are several whip handlers, you should have sufficient spotters to make sure no one walks into harm's way. Some coaches are comfortable handling half a dozen folks cracking away at the same time, but when I give a lesson or demo, I prefer to be in control of the environment, for safety's sake.

Do you have liability insurance? Check out
https://www.specialtyinsuranceagency.com/performer-insurance.html
https://www.kandkinsurance.com/Entertainment/Pages/Entertainers-Performers.aspx
http://www.shoffdarby.com/entertainment-insurance/performers
http://www.nafaa.org/fire_ins.html

Start using the whip immediately to get people used to the sound, as you talk about things. The drone of words alone can get so boring that when you get to the hands-on stage, the audience is asleep.

Target your class. For example, I start every workshop by asking folks to raise their hands to show me who is a beginner, who is intermediate, and who is advanced. This indicates to me how I should tailor my presentation so the most people will get the most benefit.

Use tricks and demonstrations to give your words reality. You must keep the interest of the audience. If they are falling asleep, they are not learning a thing.

You can demonstrate what is possible with a whip, both positive and negative, by doing tricks to demonstrate principles.

More than anything, know your material inside out. Review the videos that are out there, and the published material. If you see something you can use, use it, remembering to give proper attribution (karma's a bitch).

What you are teaching is not only how to handle a whip but also the right attitude behind its enhanced use. Get straight with yourself and whatever Higher Powers you honor before you step in front of people.

Be honest. If you don't know the answer, say so. They will respect you more for this than if you give them inaccurate information. No one person knows it all, and no amount of arrogance or egoism can obscure this simple truth from those who have eyes to see.

Keep water and snacks on hand. Teaching can be thirsty and intense work. You will be working your tail off, but it's worth the effort.

Many do this for free, some charge. There is nothing wrong with this. I heard about a patient who looked at his surgery bill and asked his doctor why his fee was so high if he was in the operating room for only three hours. The doctor replied, "You're not paying for three hours. You're paying for my years of college and medical schools, my residencies and internships, my experience and knowledge." It's a good argument!

I sometimes waive my fee and do workshops for cost, and I am happy to do this. I even do a few freebies on stage every year to give back to the Universe what the whips have given to me. I wish I could do this all the time, but airlines charge for tickets, hotels charge for rooms, restaurants charge for meals, and back home, the rent comes due and bills need to be paid. As Jimmy Durante said, "Them's the conditions that prevails!"

The best teaching tool you have is your own example. Your students will model their behaviors after yours at first, for better or for worse, so make sure you don't do anything you wouldn't want them to do. You are the living picture of whip cracking for them to watch and copy. Your students will do what they see, not what you say.

## Teaching Tips

When you are teaching, either to a group or to an individual, use these seven tools to get your message across:

**1. Be clear.** Have your student repeat or show you what you have explained. You'll see quickly enough whether or not they have it. Be willing to explain Why as much as How.

**2. Be consistent.** Repeat yourself again and again, if you have to. Don't worry about sounding like a broken record. You might be hearing yourself say something for the thousandth time, but the person standing beside you may be hearing it for the first time. Give it a chance to sink in.

**3. Think big.** Be obvious, exaggerate your motions. You can show them how to refine the moves into more subtle actions later, once they understand the principles.

**4. Make it easy for the student to make mistakes.** This makes it easier for them to solve their own problems and to move int the right motions. You are teaching them to teach themselves after you leave. Your goal is to truly teach your student, not for them to merely look good for you (or to make you look good). They will be thinking at a thousand miles an hour to begin with, and with this activity too much thinking can get in the way. Humor helps to remove this stress. If you are so good you never screw up, go ahead and screw up a little bit deliberately. Then laugh it off and do it right. They will learn from seeing you laugh and forgive yourself before you perform the move correctly.

**5. Give positive feedback.** Give negative feedback one time out of a hundred. Make the other 99 comments positive ones. You can always find something to encourage, some slight improvement that shows the person is listening and genuinely trying. If they are giving themselves to the study of this activity, you owe it to them to help them fly. Make this feedback immediate so its momentum can be taken into the next moment. The folks who are smiling are learning more than the frowners. Use lots of vocal reinforcement ("That's it! Good!")

**6. Keep it interesting.** Your student is burning a lot of energy concentrating. Focusing intensely is hard work. This can be draining, and boredom can set in. Break down problematic moves into their component actions – but then give it a break with something more easily attainable. They can come back to the problem later with a fresh mind. This will vary from student to student. One size does not fit all. Someone with martial arts or Tai Chi in their background will have an easier time of it than someone who never practiced such disciplines. Use frequent rests as rewards. Latent learning is a reality. Sometimes it just takes a little time to sink in.

**7. Make the goal Progress, not Perfection.** This saves time and will spare you and the student much agony. A beginner will never be perfect. Give them the freedom to learn. A student will hang in there long enough to get good at it if they are not hamstrung by frustration and discouragement, so give your student a history of success by presenting attainable short-term goals in small increments of difficulty. This will build their feelings of competence and confidence.

The best thing you can teach someone is how to watch themselves without judgment so they can listen to (and feel) their whips and become self-correcting and self-teaching.

This is self-serving, because this is the student who will make you look like a good teacher, even though they're doing most of the physical work. If you're doing this, you are a good teacher.

There is no need to apologize for being a good teacher or coach, or for being compensated fairly for teaching, since what you have to offer is valuable. Don't be shy about admitting this truth. As they say in Texas, "It ain't brag if it's fact!"

As a teacher, it's your job to be a voracious student on behalf of the people you teach. Watch other whip crackers, learn from everyone you can, from dancers to athletes to actors. You are learning not just for yourself, but to pass on what you've learned to others. Become the teacher you wish you'd had when you were staring out.

Arrogance results in the blind leading the blind, someone who can do two cracks lording it over those who can perform only one crack. This is a shame, because it is so unnecessary.

Within the parameters of copyright laws, feel free to pass on to others whatever you think may be useful from this book. I have no claim on the truth, but you should make sure that the truth you pass on is your own, honestly earned.

You may even show me something I have not considered. And we will both smile, because a pleasure shared is always twice the pleasure.

## Chapter 12 — In the Whip Zone

In days of old, a pirate captain would write a Final letter to his crew, to be read to them if he should not come through the fray safely. I suppose this could be such a letter to you.

I do not have all the answers. No one does. So other experienced whip handlers may suggest you do things differently. That's fine. Just take what you can use and file the rest away for later. Nothing human is written in stone.

Learn to trust the whip. It does not lie. There is no ego in the Power Wave.

The whip has certainly been uncompromising to me in its honest and immediate feedback. Its direct reality has grounded me and illuminated my path for years. My desire is to do it honor by sharing with you what I know of it.

That being said, this book is not intended to be an encyclopedia. It is not a comprehensive reference work, and it absolutely is not the last word on the subject.

I agree with metaphysical author Dion Fortune, who defined Magic as the art of changing consciousness at will. In short, Magic is Power — and for me, the bullwhip is power made conscious and tangible. Each crack is a wake-up call, an affirmation, a step in the dance of life and death, at the same instant glorious, graceful and terrifying. Further, it's sexy, it's scary, and it's dangerous — and it's fun.

So here is a book to serve the Sorcerer's Apprentice, and I hope it is also a book against which other masters of the whip may compare their knowledge.

I do not pretend to have created any of the material in this book, any more than Edison "invented" electricity. All I have done is to pull together what I've learned from others and what I've been taught by my own direct experience with the whip — but it is still only one man's perspective.

In this world there are many people well qualified to address this subject. The Internet has made many of these people immediately accessible to almost everyone. Some are expert handlers, some are whip braiders, some are top-notch teachers. Most are workers, while some are wizards. With only a few exceptions, they all have something to share and teach.

Obviously, this book is written from a whip cracker's view, not a whip maker's. There are several excellent books showing how to braid a whip, but not that many that show how to crack a whip. Even today, there are only two other credible books easily available in the US that address whip cracking itself. The first is "The Filipino Fighting Whip," by Tom Meadows, which treats whip cracking as a martial art. The second is the one written by my friend Andrew Conway, "The Bullwhip Book." It is a measure of his generosity of spirit that he has been so helpful in the writing of this volume.

Talking about whips is always difficult, because there is no common vocabulary worldwide for cracks or even whips. Often the differences between differently named whips and cracks are maddeningly miniscule.

I've spoken with many experienced coaches, leather braiders and performers about their experiences with bullwhips, and without exception, we were able to communicate and understand each other because this is a language based in experience, not theory.

So the more I learn, the more I see how much more there is to learn. A good teacher never stops being a student. A good magician never believes he knows it all.

The list of folks to thank is a long one, but without each one of them this book would not have happened:

I thank Gery Deer, a gentleman, entertainer and teacher, for his generosity and respect. I thank Chris Camp for his stolid camaraderie. And I thank Brian Chic for his friendship and example, and for reminding me at a timely moment in my life that teaching must always be a two-way street for it to have any value.

I wish I could thank everyone who has contributed to this. A mere list would be inadequate., but any list would always include Joe Wheeler, Mike Murphy, Peter Jack, Mark Allen, Alex Green, Russell Schultz, Sharron Taylor, Rhett Kelley and Guy Baldwin.

I thank the late Ken Fontenot, Col. Niabow, and Michael A., for first opening my eyes to what was possible with a bullwhip years ago in Houston, Texas. I thank Chris Wiggins and Brenda Fogg for their faith, their friendship, and a shared passion for sushi.

Philip Miller and Molly Devon are to be thanked for first encouraging me to commit my thoughts to paper. And patient Molly should be thanked again for encouraging me to complete this project.

I thank Jay Wagner of Toronto for being the first person to ask me to bring my whips to a fundraiser, whetting an appetite in me to pursue a career as a bullwhip artist.

I thank John Brady (and Vi) for setting the standard and blazing a trail around the globe which others now follow. I thank Alan Fox for helping me to create the ground-breaking video, "Bullwhip: Art of the Single Tail Whip." I sincerely thank Loup and Jan of Portland for their steadfast friendship in whip craft.

I thank everyone who ever attended a practice sponsored by the Los Angeles Whip Enthusiasts. I also thank the incredible attendees of The Minneapolis Bullwhip Academy who braved hell, high water and snow drifts to join me cracking whips in studios in the Twin Cities.

I thank Paul Nolan, Drew, Dorothy M., Stephanie, Don Bastian, Karen Quest, Joyce Rice, Mitch Herman_(and Kathleen), Manon_(and Jessica), and Rob M. for sharing their time and invaluable insights with me.

I thank Mark Shuler, a man who knows there need be no discrepancy between sensitivity and courage, who helped me cross the Rubicon to my first Guinness World Record.

I thank those whose names I have forgotten, even to the 5-year-old kids who showed me things I hadn't seen before.

I wish to thank again Andrew Conway, whose own book, "The Bullwhip Book," has helped this art and sport reach a wider audience. His patient, painstaking reading of my manuscript and his suggestions (especially in the chapters on performing) were invaluable. Happily, he is as good a teacher as he is a friend, so I count myself doubly blessed to know him. Thank you, Andrew!

I thank Paul McDonald, whose sharp-eyed reading encouraged me to improve the quality of the final version of this book. I also thank Carl Bergstrom.

I thank Mike Woolridge for epitomizing all that's good and true about "The Cowboy Way."

I wish to thank Drs. John Bartlett and Tom Walsh. I thank Dr. Sharon Young, whose voice I still hear in moments of lucidity and compassion. I thank my father, an RAF navigator who taught me how to look at the stars; I thank my mother, who showed me how to make a cup of tea as though this mundane act held secrets of profound meaning (it does!); I thank my brother Ronald, a true modern day buccaneer; I thank Allen Ginsberg who gave me friendship and good advice (to this day I think he should have been awarded a Nobel Prize for so many different and legitimate reasons); and I thank Nutmeg, a little fellow who showed me the meaning of 'unconditional love,' and that without it, no one can hope to fully embrace the human experience.

To this roster we should add the following names: Wayde Allen, Chris and Brenda Wiggins, Anthony and Mary DeLongis, Mike Murphy, Joe Wheeler, Peter Jack, Gayle Nemeth, Guy Baldwin, Sharron Taylor, Jan and Loup, Drew, David Morgan, Ron Edwards and Ernst Mach. And I thank Tina Nagy/Ritt,_under whose roof the first book was written.

And last, but not least, I thank the irrepressible Mary Dante, my partner, my friend, my wife and my traveling companion in this journey between worlds. Thanks to you, Mary, "I am full."

I hope, with this book, I've given back to the whips some small measure of what they have given me over the enchanted years. As I've already said, any and all errors in here are my own.

While a book, a hands-on lesson, or a good video can teach technique, it cannot communicate that intangible 'Spirit of the Whip.' All I can do is point.

It's an Open Secret, as Rumi said. The magic is already in your hand, waiting for you to free it — and for it to free you.

— Robert Dante —

## TWO PRACTICE ROUTINES

**Practice Routine No. 1 – Basic Cracks**

**A. Setting the Whip**
**B. Overhand Flick**
**C. Circus Crack**
**D. Stockman's Crack**

(For right-handed people, the dominant side is the right side; the weak side is left side. For lefties, the left side is the dominant side; the right side is the weak side. Please wear eye protection.)

**A. Setting the Whip**

1. Kneel on one knee. Roll the whip out in front of you with your dominant hand. Roll the whip back behind you. Make sure the line is straight and the whip does not "slap" the floor.

2. Roll the whip out with your dominant hand on the other side of your body, straight in front, then straight behind you.

3. Switch hands. Roll the whip with your weak hand on the weak side of your body, laying it out straight in front, then straight behind.

4. Use your weak hand to roll the whip out on the dominant side of your body, straight out in front, then straight out behind you.

5. Stand. Repeat the above moves while standing instead of kneeling.

## B. Overhand Flick

1. Throw the whip forward gently with your dominant hand on your dominant side. After it cracks, cycle the whip down in an arc passing by your dominant side until it is behind you and primed to be thrown forward again.

2. Cycle the whip on your weak side with your dominant hand.

3. Switch hands and do steps 1 and 2 with your weak hand on both sides of your body.

4. Alternate sides so you are making swash buckler-type cross cuts. Make the cracks occur at the same point directly in front of you, so the whip is following an X-shaped trajectory in front of you.

## C. Circus Crack

1. Do a circus crack with your dominant hand on your dominant side, then ground the whip on your dominant side.

2. Do a circus crack with your dominant hand on your weak side, then ground the whip on your weak side.

3. Switch hands. Do circus crack with weak hand on weak side (grounding to the weak side), then with weak hand on dominant side (grounding to the dominant side).

## D. Cattleman's Crack

1. Pull the whip up on your dominant side with your dominant hand as if you are doing a circus crack, but angle the whip's trajectory above your head, crack going away from you, and then follow through outside your body. Repeat, increasing the angle of attack slightly until the whole stroke is almost parallel to the ground.

2. Switch hands. Repeat the step above, but with your weak hand on your weak side.

## Practice Routine No. 2 – Multiple Cracks

A. Slow Figure 8s
B. Fast Figure 8s
C. Volleys
D. Self Wraps

### A. Slow Figure 8s

1. Perform a forward circus crack on your dominant side with your dominant hand. As you follow through, swing the whip up behind you into a reverse circus crack. Use the next sweep-through to line the whip up for your next forward circus crack.

2. Switch hands. Do the same move on your weak side with your weak hand.

3. Mix it up – dominant hand on weak side, weak hand on dominant side.

### B. Fast Figure 8s

1. Do a Circus Crack on your dominant side. Immediately after it cracks and before it continues down in front of you, roll the whip handle backward and pull it into a small vertical circular loop going clockwise. Use the sweep-through after this second crack to line the whip up for your next forward Circus Crack.

2. Switch hands. Repeat the motion with your weaker hand.

### C. Volleys

1. On your dominant side, do one crack forward, one crack behind, like a fast Figure 8, then sweep the whip under and up to start the next volley. This is a two-crack volley.

2. See if you can increase the number of times you can make it crack in a continuous move, up to 12.

3. Switch hands.

## SAFETY PROTOCOLS

*(These are safety protocols devised by Andrew Conway for use at the San Francisco Circus Arts School. They are reprinted here with his kind permission.)*

Bullwhips can cut flesh, break bones, put out eyes, slice ears and cheeks. Treat whips with respect and use these common sense precautions to limit the damage to an occasional welt.

**Protect Other People**

Be aware of the space around you, including directly behind you and over your head. Allow plenty of room for your whip to crack.

Do not fool around with a whip or threaten anyone with it. Uncontrolled and unscripted use of a whip can have unpredictable results.

Never use a whip where it can pick up dirt or gravel and fling it at someone.

**Protect Yourself**

Wear protective clothing. Eye protection is required. Gloves will prevent blisters on your hands. Ear plugs will make the sound level more comfortable. A stout jacket and pants may save you some welts.

When you are not cracking, stay near the walls of the gym. Do not enter anyone else's space without warning them. Remember they may wearing ear plugs, so make sure they acknowledge you.

**Protect the Whips**

Do not crack the whip too loud. It is bad for the whip and unpleasant for other people. True control of the whip means you can crack it as quietly as you want.

Do not use anyone else's whip without permission.

When you are not using the whip, do not leave it on the floor where someone might tread on it or trip over it.

# CAN KIDS CRACK WHIPS?

If kids can learn karate, soccer, or other "adult" sports, they can also learn to handle bullwhips and stock whips safely and expertly.

Some of the best whip crackers in history were smaller men and women. To crack a whip powerfully, accurately and dramatically does not require a great deal of strength. If the form is correct, the physics of the whip will allow the cracker to reach supersonic speeds with relatively little effort.

In Australia, kids enter junior whip handling competitions at county fairs. I have several videos of this. Mike Murphy, the world famous whip maker and whip cracker, sells a video showing Andrew Thomas, the champion whip cracker, performing routines with an 8-year old Daniel Wicks doing precisely the same moves right beside him. Yes, the boy's whips are shorter, but he holds his own. He will be a great ambassador for whip cracking in the future!

The United States is far behind Australia in this sport, but interest is growing. Since the Australians have codified criteria for objectively judging whip routines and competitions, the back-scene buzz is that someday whip cracking will be an Olympic sport.

What are the benefits such instruction can give a child? Just as many as karate_or soccer_can offer a kid!

A youngster's confidence_grows as he or she sees that the whip will crack, almost magically, by itself. This is a lot of power for a child to control, the sort of thing kids have been jazzed about for years.

In the Victorian era, children used whips to keep tops spinning as a game. Even today, if I practice in a park, it's the little ones who drag their parents over to watch!

Whip cracking teaches youngsters to have confidence, self discipline, the philosophy of "less is more," and an understanding of logical consequences. It gives a sense of camaraderie to youths_-_once a child masters a move they first desire to show off. They then try to teach the move to others.

In many ways it is easier to teach kids than adults. Kids don't intellectualize what they're doing. They just do it.

To get adults into this open-minded "child's" way of learning, I have them work with their weaker hands where they are more awkward. This forces them to listen to their bodies and to pay attention to the reality of the moment like children. They are less likely to compare what's happening with some ideal image of how things "ought" to be. When they go back to using their dominant hands, they are amazed to see how much their weaker hands have taught them.

People enjoy this as a sport for its own sake, feeling the satisfaction of resounding and graceful cracks coming from the whips in their hands.

People still enjoy the sport of archery, although we no longer have to kill wild game to eat. We enjoy martial arts_like karate_and kendo, though the age of the samurai_is past. And while there aren't too many cattle drives through the hearts of cities, anymore, there are whip cracking clubs in urban areas. Cracking whips makes kids of us all, so it's natural that kids enjoy this sport!

# FREQUENTLY ASKED QUESTIONS

These are the six questions I am often asked. They are answered elsewhere in this book, but I've put them in this section apart for easy reference :

- "What are the parts of the bullwhip called?"

- "How do you tie a cracker onto the fall?"

- "How often should I condition my whip -- and what should I use?"

- "Can I really swing on a bullwhip like Indiana Jones?"

- "What's the single best source for information about bullwhips?"?

- "Did you ever hit yourself? And did it hurt?"?

- "What is the speed of sound?"

**"What are the parts of the bullwhip called?"**

See Chapter 1 - Whips

**"How do you tie a cracker to the fall?"**

See Chapter 6 - Poppers

**"What is the best material to use for a cracker?"**

Good question! I cannot say there is any one "best" material for a cracker. They all have their plusses and minuses.

Personally, for everyday use, I use mason's twine from hardware stores. I can skin it down to the thinness I want, I can choose my own colors (lighter for darker rooms) and it is not cost-prohibitive. I also use embroidery thread, which is durable and makes a sharp crack.

I've been given some human hair to see what I can do with it, and that experiment is still going on. I have used horsehair, silk, polyester thread, twine, fishing line, etc.

After choosing the material, I look at the end use of the cracker -- will I be performing soft wraps around a finger, or do I need to be able to slice a banana, or do I want a LOUD crack with the least effort. This allows me to make the cracker that will most suit the purpose, because when you make your own crackers, you have a lot of control over that aspect of your whip's performance.

The key, whatever the material, is make it as tightly as possible so it will carry the energy wave without losing power due to internal friction. Here's how: Figure out how long and how thick you want the final cracker. However many strands you decide on, the cracker will be one-quarter of the length of the original strands and four times as thick.

Make a loop (add a knot), put a chopstick through each end of the loop and start twisting one while you anchor the other one between your knees. When it is tight as a guitar string and won't go any tighter without starting to double on itself, pinch the center of the twirled string and pull toward yourself, allowing the two chopsticks to rest against each other.

When you let go of the string, it will spring into action and become your cracker. Add the knot wherever you want, making the fuzzy part as short or long as you like -- or as I often do, snip it half and half for a two-tone crack. Trim off the excess (such as the original knot when you made the loop). You're ready to go.

If I want something more aerodynamic, I will tie the cracker's knot in a fisherman's double hitch, making the knot smoother and smaller.

When in doubt, remember that tighter is always better. It's all about the physics.

**"How often should I condition my whip, and what should I use?"**

The whip itself will tell you when it needs a dose. It doesn't go by the calendar.

Condition your whip when it feels relatively dry and stiff. Don't overcondition it, because this will weaken the strands over time.

Usually, the fall requires conditioning more often than the thong. Wipe on, leave it for a few minutes, then wipe off with a soft rag, stroking from the handle toward the lash.

You do not need to condition the whole whip every time you do it -- just the end. The handle is rarely conditioned.

As for which product, there are many good choices out there. You can use Blackrock Leather 'N' Rich, Pecards, Fiebings, Jay-El, or Dr. Jackson's Hide Rejuvenator. (Pro whip handler Joyce Rice told me she used dish soap for its lanolin!)

By the way, more than once I heard from old cowboys that the sweat on your hands is the best grease.

Whatever you do,_DO NOT_use Neatsfoot Oil! It chemically "burns" leather the way gasoline will burn your bare arm.

**"Can I really swing on a bullwhip like Indiana Jones?"**

No!

Swinging from a whip will stretch the leather, making your whip wrinkle up like taffeta afterward.
The whips used in the Indiana Jones movies have nylon rope cores or aircraft cable with an overlay of kangaroo.

They are made specifically for swinging, not for cracking._It's a great fantasy, but reality is elsewhere.

Simply put, swinging on it will kill your whip. Don't do it.

**"What's the single best source for information about bullwhips?"**

There are three good ones. You're holding the first one: "Let's Get Cracking: The How-To Book of Bullwhip Skills."

Second, I recommend Ron Edwards' book, "How To Make Whips". You can get a copy at Amazon.com.

And third, I strongly suggest you bookmark_The Bullwhip FAQ. Started by whip teacher and author Andrew Conway years ago, it's been continually updated. The information is good and the writing is interesting.

**"Did you ever hit yourself? And did it hurt?"**

Yes! And yes, again! As I am fond of saying, "Show me a juggler who never dropped a ball, and I'll show you a whip cracker who never hit her/himself."

When you're learning (or even when you've got a lot of experience), there will be the occasional misthrow. You will get whacked.

This is why I urge folks to wear eye protection (safety glasses), long sleeves, and a hat with a brim (to protect the ears and nose).

And yes, of course it hurts! Sometimes it's a sting, sometimes it's a smack, and sometimes it's a good wallop. This is why I urge you to use safety protocols.

Incidentally, when you hear the crack of the whip, the energy is expended. This means if you get hit after it cracks, the injury will probably be minor -- but it can still hurt! However, if the whip's lash hits you before the whip has cracked, all that pent-up energy will go right into your body -- and that means you may be looking at a welt or a bruise. We live in a world of logical consequences!

**"What is the Speed of Sound?"**

What is the Speed of Sound? In a sea-level atmosphere at 20°C (68°F), the speed of sound is 761 mph (1,225 km/h) or 1100 feet a second. That's ten times faster than freeway speed in the U.S.
That's faster than most passenger jets. A stronger crack can reach 900 mph, even up to Mach 2. The actual duration of a sonic boom is brief; less than a second, 100 milliseconds (0.1 second).

## *GETTING READY FOR SPRING*

When the long winter is almost over, like most folks we are ready to get out onto green grass with our whips. Here are four steps to get a good start on a new year's positive whip cracking experience:

4. Condition your whips, if they need it (I recommend Fiebing's Leather Conditioner). Use this as an opportunity to reacquaint yourself with your whips. Look for signs of wear. Put on fresh crackers. Replace falls, if necessary.

5. When you get out there, remember to warm up, first. Start slowly and include stretching in the process, before you get into the rhythm of the whips.

6. Make sure the turf is right. The ground might still be soggy, even if the grass is coming in strong, and water and leather don't mix (nylon whip users can ignore this item). Plus, your whip does not like the beach or your asphalt driveway. The driveway scrapes your whip like sandpaper; the beach gets grains of sand into your whip which then work like tiny saws weakening your whip. We won't even talk about sand in your eyes when the wind changes direction!

7. Which brings us to this: Don't forget to bring your safety glasses and a hat with a brim! When you were born, God gave you two eyes, and you don't get any more than that, so take care of them. Expect the unexpected, whether you are a beginner or an experienced whip handler.

The result of doing these steps will be more enjoyment and more safety for you, and a longer and livelier life for your whips.

## SAMPLE SCRIPTS

**Devil's Tower Show**
20 minutes – Deadwood Stage :39
Intro - Juniper – 3:21
Flash/Chop Lop - Celtic– 2:40
Horse - Dangerous – 1:00
DinoTail - Penn Rose – 1:21
Intro Mary- Morocco - :15
Balloon Time #1 - Bandit – 0:48
Newspaper cut w/ Stamp
    Crisis – 1:29
Balloon Time #2 - Bandit – 0:48
Candles & Tiki Torch - Chase – 2:15
Styro, Wraps, Double Whips
    Noble Race – 5:18
Ending/farewell
Balloon Time #3 - Bandit – 0:48
    Achaidh Cheide – 2:14

**Intro**
From Herdsmen to Horsemen
Whips used as weapons and working tools - And Entertainment.

**Flash opening**
It slices, it dices,
It chops, it lops, it crops -
It skewers and "spewers" –
T: That's not a word!
R: Feldercarb! I thought it was!

**Ground Zero**
3 sets    5 minutes each

**SET 1**
Music    4:24
Dangerous – Sellisternia

**Props - 1**
Balloon belt
Balloons
Styrofoam strips
2 Styrofoam strip holsters
Sound Equipment

**Routine**
Intro to whip - R
Balloon pops – M
    Hand-held & with belt
Styrofoam strips
   (End with Cut Throat)

*****

**SET 2**
Music    4:30
Stratosphere – Dark Dance

**Props - 2**
Blindfold
Styrofoam strips
Candles handheld
Tea lights
Magician's wax
Lighter
newspaper

Routine
Newspaper
Hand candles
Tea lights
Blindfold

*****
**SET 3**
Music   4:30
Totentanz

**Props 3**
Blacklight whips
Blacklights & cords
Surge protector

Reg whip wraps
UV whip wraps


**A Standard Ending**
    You may wonder why we do this, why we perform with whips.
    Do people crack whips because it's a piece of living history?
    Both: NO!!
    Do we crack whips because it is a martial art so difficult to master that only a very few people can actually get good with it?
    Both: NO!!
    Do we do it because it's dangerous?
    R: NO!!
    M: YES!!
    (Double take)
    Do we do it because it's fun?
    Both: Yes!!
    R: I'm Robert Dante, this is Mary, and We both wish you a Good Night!


**Shooters Roundup**

**Music – Action- Props**
1 Trailer- Seating-warmup-greeting
2 Western streets- whips-mach one- 3 whips
3 sting 1- Tina intro
4 sting 2- Tina solo
5 gold rush 1- balloon miss 1   - balloons
6 hand trolley- card trick- deck, large card
7 Shanty- poi – newspaper- poi – newspaper
8 Waltz- mirror cut- flower – mirror
9 gold rush 2- balloon miss 2- balloon
10 Smoking gun- dinosaur story- snake whip – maracas
11 Tango- Whip duet

12 Dangerous- Swashbucklers
13 Penn Rose- farewells, advertising
14 gold rush 3- balloon hit 3- balloons
15 Doris Day- Finale

**A Standard Opening**

When you hear the whip crack, it is breaking the Sound Barrier at 761 mph. That's 1100 feet a second. A bullet leaves the barrel of a gun at 850 feet a sec, so the whip is actually going faster than a bullet. At that speed, things could get dangerous, so let's hope I'm accurate tonight.

**Whip Cliches**
- "I can flick a fly from the ear of my lead horse without making him break his stride!"
- "Neither you nor your chariot will ever be the equal of Masallah, Judah Ben Hur!"
- "Row, English Dogs! The King himself has special plans for you when we get back to Spain!"
- "Roy, those bandits have almost caught up with us and we're still 10 miles away from the fort!"
- "Well, Meow! Where are you going, Batman?"
- "Tie me kangaroo down, sport! I'll meet you over by the billabong!"
- "My name is Inigo Montoya. You killed my father. Prepare to die!"

**The Dinosaur Story**

Sixty-five million years ago, there lived a gigantic dinosaur, we later called the Apatosaurus. Or the Brontosaurus. Turns out they were the same animal.

This creature was 95 feet long, and 45 feet of it was its tail, which it flicked back and forth as it walked, cracking it like a bullwhip.

Scientists have since determined that the animals with tails that could crack were all male (they looked at the bones in the hips, or something).

Now, Nature has a creature draw attention itself like this for one of three reasons:
The first reason is a territorial one: "If you can hear this, you're too close."
The second reason is a Macho intimidation: "My crack is bigger than yours."
The third reason is that it's a mating call.
(Crack whip – Assistant comes running)
Sixty-five million years later, and things have not changed!

### The Fly Story
When I was in Texas, I went out to see an old rancher about his oil lease.

He saw that I had a bullwhip on my back seat, and he asked, "You any good with that?"

I lied and said, "Yep, I sure am!"

He reached for his own bullwhip there on the porch, saying "We'll see."

Now, this was Texas in the summer. The horse flies were buzzing around big as quarters. He nodded, and I knew what he meant. I picked out my fly, and as it buzzed by, I snapped the bullwhip out there.

The fly exploded like he had hit a windshield!

I turned around and said proudly, "There!" I did not tell him it was 99 percent luck on my part, but I took credit anyway.

"Pretty good," he said. "Let's see what I can do."

He picked out a fly. Buzz buzz buzz it came. The whip snapped out – Pow! - and the fly buzzed on, unconcerned.

"Aha!" I cried. "You missed!"

"No, no!" he said. "That fly will never have children!"

### Second Standard Opening
A whip crack is a sonic boom. The end of the whip accelerates as it rolls out, and as it passes 761 miles per hour -- I'm sorry, we're in Canada so that's 1224.71 kilometers per hour -- it breaks the sound barrier. That's nearly seven times the speed of a sneeze, which is 100 mph!

For those of you with calculators, that's 1100 feet per second! In Annie Oakley's day, a bullet left the barrel of a gun at 850 feet per second, so you can see that the lash of the whip is actually going faster than a bullet. That makes it dangerous; or for folks like us, that's what makes it fun! So let's get started...!

### Patter Before Popping a Balloon
Once, across this land, there were mighty, thundering herds of balloons.

And then came the bullwhip.

The bullwhip shattered the little water balloons, but the herd of the Tough Latex went against the bullwhip, and it beat itself stupid trying to pop them.

To this day, they are sworn enemies.

Now we reenact one of the battles of that great conflict!

### For Indiana Jones Audience - Story 1
The Bullwhip symbolizes Adventure, Danger. Depending on who is holding it, the bullwhip can be a weapon, or a tool, or a toy.

And thanks to the character Indiana Jones, 35 years ago the United States rediscovered the bullwhip.

Whips are found in all cultures, in all ages of history. They've been found in the graves of neanderthal hunters. Pictures of them are on the walls of the pyramids in Egypt.

Today, they are still used around the world as tools to extend authority over animals at a distance. Even the Eskimos use whips to encourage their sled dogs.

None of the folks who use whips actually hit animals with them. Cowboys who used whips to herd cattle would never want an angry cow on their hands, and they sure wouldn't want to bruise the meat or cut the leather. So they'd crack their whips and the animals would move in the opposite direction.

You'll find bullwhips today at Wild West shows, in circuses, at science fiction conventions – and in the movies.

Bullwhips have been cracked in the movies since the days of silent films. Douglas Fairbanks, the old Zorro...new Zorro, Antonio Banderas and Anthony Hopkins...Catwoman, Underworld.

Happily, Harrison Ford actually knows how to crack a whip. The whips used in the Indiana Jones movies were made by David Morgan, Joe Strain, and for the last one, Terry Jakka of Australia.

### For Indiana Jones Audience Story 2 - David Morgan's Whips

The Indiana Jones whip was No. 453 (8 ft. length) or the No. 455 (10 ft. length), was incorporated into the story by the first stunt coordinator, Glenn Randall.

David Morgan sent six bullwhips to the Raiders production team, and this led to his later supplying more than 30 bullwhips of the 450 series for the Indiana Jones films, from six feet to 16 feet long. The standard length seen in the movies was the No. 455 10-foot whip. Other special whips were made for specific scenes, like the metal cable-core whip with the leather overlay, used to drag Indy behind the speeding truck. These whips were not made for cracking. (This particular whip was owned by Kit West, the mechanical effects director on the film, and was later auctioned for $61,000.)

### For Indiana Jones Audience - Story 3

Some years back, Maxim Magazine asked Harrison Ford, "Is there a practical use for a bullwhip?"

Ford said, "It depends on your girlfriend."

## WHIP REPAIR KIT

Keep a specific bag or cigar box (or something similar or personal) with your whips and bring it with you everywhere you travel with your whips. Make them inseparable.

Here's what you'll find in my own sturdy and scuffed 1930s Montgomery Ward fishing tackle box:

- string to make poppers
- chopsticks (or any other straight objects like pencils or crochet needles) for twisting poppers
- paramedic scissors (inexpensive, but they'll cut anything, even leather), and/or a good knife
- extra falls - any whip maker will sell you some. Expect to pay $5 to $10.
- lots of extra poppers, already braided (when you need a new one, you need it NOW, not later)
- Band Aids because hey, sometimes stuff happens
- antibiotic ointment (see above)
- extra safety glasses - if someone wants to join you or you're showing someone how to do a new crack
- needle nose pliers
- hemostats
- dentist's pick
- fid, which is a leather working tool like an awl – great for loosening up tight knots without injuring the leather

When folks are cracking their whips together, these are the items they'll usually borrow from each other (so you might want to put in an extra cigar for a friend). If you've got your own kit together, you'll be able to handle just about anything that might come up in the course of a practice session.

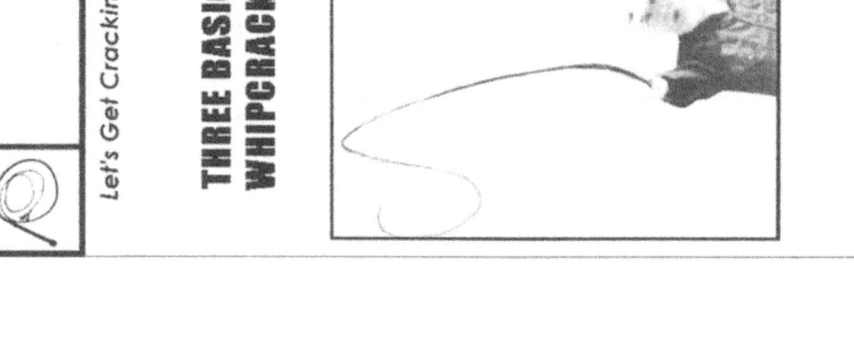

*Let's Get Cracking!*

# THREE BASIC WHIPCRACKS

**DANTE'S BULLWHIPS**
**Robert Dante**

---

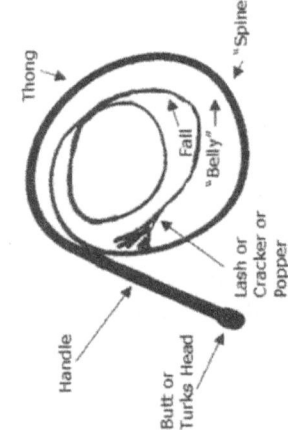

**DANTE'S BULLWHIPS**
**Robert Dante**

E-mail: dante@bullwhip.net
HTTP://BULLWHIP.NET

© Robert Dante

---

### SAFETY FIRST
Always protect your eyes. Wear protection. A hat with a brim will help protect your nose and ears.

### "RAILROAD TRACKS"
Imagine you are standing between railroad tracks. If you are inside the tracks and the whip is outside the tracks, you will not get hit, even when the whip is behind you. Keep your elbow inside the tracks.

### BELLY UP
Position "belly" to top of hand, so whip travels in loop outside your forearm. Whip loop travels straight and tight along belly-spine axis.

### ANATOMY OF A WHIP

**Butt or Turks Head**
Knot at end of whip
**Handle**
Long-handled whips are called "Target Whips"
**Thong**
Braided length between handle and fall
**Fall**
Lace from thong to cracker. Easy to replace
**Lash or Cracker or Popper**
String on end of whip that makes noise.
**"Belly" and "Spine"**
Belly is inside curl of whip; Spine is outside curl. Whip wants to roll along this axis.

# 1
## The Circus Crack

This is often the easiest crack to learn.

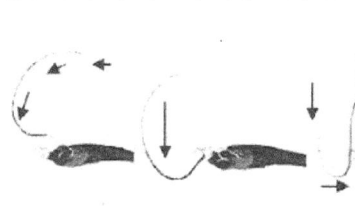

Swing the whip up into the air over your head. Feel the tug of the cracker.

While the whip is traveling backward over your shoulder, push the whip forward under the backward path. Your hand should make a little circle, like the drive arm of a train.

The whip will form an S-shape as it catches up with itself. The loop will roll forward.

Aim and squeeze. You can tell the whip where to crack.

*TIPS:*

Keep elbow in, forearm straight up, like a sword fighter. This keeps handle parallel to your body, and the whip follows the handle on a straight line.

Go Big and Slow — If you go big, you can go slow and not lose power. You will gain in accuracy and control. Use a lot of shoulder, a bit of elbow, and almost no wrist until the final "point and squeeze." Aim down your arm and handle. The whip will crack at 2/3 to 3/4 of its length, closer to you than other cracks.

# 2
## The Overhand Crack

Use swimming motion, extend arm, to make this work.

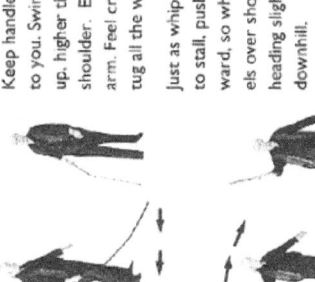

Keep handle parallel to you. Swing whip up, higher than shoulder. Extend arm. Feel cracker tug all the way up.

Just as whip begins to stall, push forward, so whip travels over shoulder, heading slightly downhill.

Aim down handle at target. Point and squeeze handle just before whip cracks. Follow through to left or right.

*TIPS:*

The rhythm is 1-2-3, with slight pause at "2."

Keep palm facing forward all the way around motion.

"Whip Throwing" is a misnomer. It's really "whip pulling" and "whip pushing." Let the whip do the work.

Whip will crack at full length of whip, making this a good crack for accuracy at a specific point in space.

Good whip crackers don't "muscle" their whips or force them to crack—They *guide* them and *let* them crack. Power is *already* in the whip.

# 3
## The Cattleman's Crack

This is just a Circus Crack on a different plane.

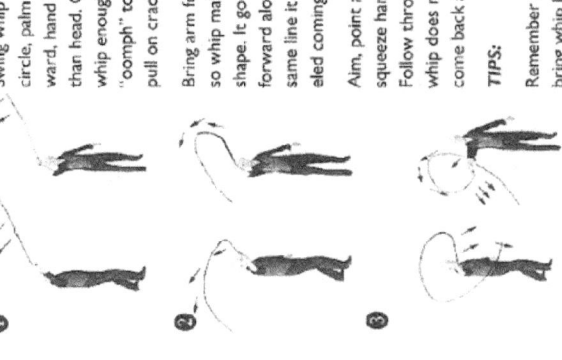

Swing whip in wide circle, palm forward, hand higher than head. Give whip enough "oomph" to feel pull on cracker.

Bring arm forward so whip makes "S" shape. It goes forward along same line it traveled coming back.

Aim, point and squeeze handle. Follow through so whip does not come back at you.

*TIPS:*

Remember to bring whip back with hand higher than head, or you will wrap your neck.

Keep rolling loop tight against whip by bringing whip forward along the same line it traveled going back. If you change direction of whip, it will not have a chance to crack—it will "waffle."

Use pectoral muscles with big sweeping motion, not wrist, as if you are removing a big sombrero.

Make sure whip comes back outside your arm. You can "hide" under your extended arm, protecting yourself.

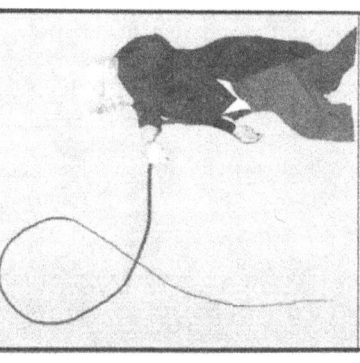

### Let's Get Cracking!
## Multiple Cracks:
## FAST FIGURE 8s, VOLLEYS & FLASHES

**DANTE'S BULLWHIPS**
Robert Dante

"*A Sequence of Multiple Cracks Is Called a FLASH.*"

A FLASH is a showy way to crack a whip. The name derives from the area where the crack originated or from the use of the crack. For example, the Queensland Flash comes from Queensland (Australia).

In the Wild West days, some stage coach drivers had particular Flashes associated with their stage lines. One sequence called the Wells Fargo Flash had 6 cracks—one for each horse. When residents of a town heard specific cracking from afar, they could tell which stage line was coming into town.

## TIMING TERMS
### *For Two-Handed Whip Cracking*

***Together Time:*** Both whips are cracked in unison, at the same time.

***Staggered Time:*** One whip lags behind the other one slightly.

***Balanced Time:*** The two whips crack alternately. For example, in a two-handed volley, the result is a steady crack-crack-crack-crack to the front, first with right hand, then left hand, then right hand, etc.

## SAFETY FIRST

Remember to protect your eyes. Always wear eye protection.

A hat with a brim will protect your nose and ears.

Long sleeves will help diminish an inadvertent whack to your forearms.

**DANTE'S BULLWHIPS**
Robert Dante
E-mail: dance@bullwhip.net
HTTP://BULLWHIP.NET

© Robert Dante

# Fast Figure 8s

Fast Figure 8's are great warm ups for Volleys, Sydney Flashes, Queensland Flashes, and other multiple-crack moves.

You will use your skill with the Overhand Flick and your ability to set your whip backward with a flick of your wrist.

Throw the whip forward in a Circus Crack. After it cracks, "bounce" the cracker backward beside you, letting it pass over the top of your hand. In other words, you throw the whip forward, then set it behind you before it hits the ground. If you do it well, you have a vertical crack forward which immediately rolls into a vertical crack behind you. There is no pause between the two cracks.

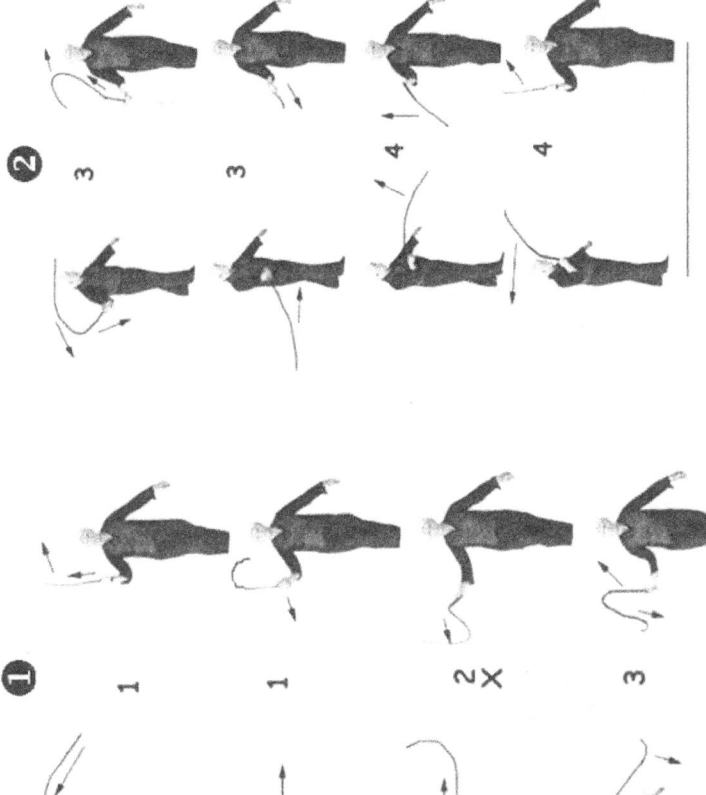

**Fast Figure 8— One Complete Cycle**
"X" is the first crack point before you pull

## QUEENSLAND FLASH

The Queensland Flash is a Fast Figure 8 followed by a Circus Crack.

To do this three-crack move, crack in front, crack behind, then crack it again as it rises in front. You can do these all day, and they are dramatic performed with two whips.

## SYDNEY FLASH

The SYDNEY FLASH is the Queensland Flash with this difference: instead of starting with a Circus Crack forward, throw an Overhand Flick.

This one is more difficult to do continuously, because your whip has to stop and change direction from the rising movement (after the third crack) in order to execute the overhand throw forward for the next Sydney Flash.

And yes, you can perform Reverse Queensland Flashes and Sydney Flashes with the first crack occurring behind you.

## VOLLEY

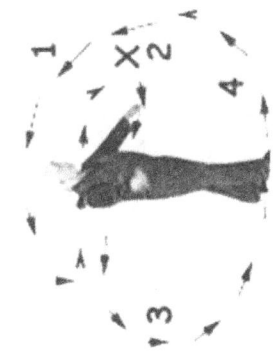

A VOLLEY is simply cracking the whip back and forth. Every crack becomes the start of the next crack. Keep the handle almost straight up, but angle the handle very slightly outward for the thong to pass by your hand.

Use your whole arm. You have more control over the line of your whip if you use your arm, not just your wrist.

When most people start a throw backward, they usually angle the handle out at 45-degrees, but this will make the whip want to gyre back at an awkward angle. Remember: the crack starts in the setup, not just in the execution. As with most activities, foreplay determines the quality of what is to follow.

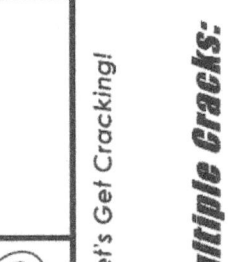

*Let's Get Cracking!*

# Multiple Cracks:
# SLOW FIGURE 8S

**DANTE'S BULLWHIPS**
**Robert Dante**

(831) 869-1717

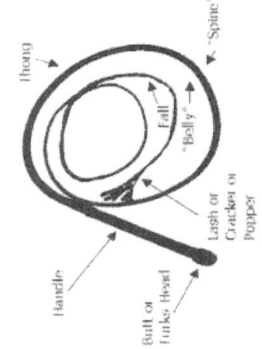

## SAFETY FIRST
Always protect your eyes. Wear protection. A hat with a brim will help protect your nose and ears.

## "RAILROAD TRACKS"
Imagine you are standing between railroad tracks. If you are inside the tracks and the whip is outside the tracks, you will not get hit, even when the whip is behind you. Keep your elbow inside the tracks.

## BELLY UP
Position "belly" to top of hand, so whip travels in loop outside your forearm. Whip loop travels straight and tight along belly-spine axis.

## ANATOMY OF A WHIP

**Butt or Turks Head**
Knot at end of whip
**Handle**
Long handled whips are called "Target Whips"
**Thong**
Braided length between handle and fall
**Fall**
Lace from thong to cracker. Easy to replace.
**Lash or Cracker or Popper**
String on end of whip that makes noise.
**"Belly" and "Spine"**
Belly is inside curl of whip; Spine is outside curl. Whip wants to roll along this axis.

**DANTE'S BULLWHIPS**
**Robert Dante**

E-mail: dance@bullwhip.net
HTTP://BULLWHIP.NET

© Robert Dante

## Slow Figure 8s

This is a marvelous exercise in combining cracks, since the cracks flow smoothly into each other.

Essentially, Slow Figure 8s are two Circus Cracks — a regular Circus Crack and a Reverse Circus Crack.

Start with a forward Circus Crack (FIG. 1). Swing the whip up into the air over your head. Feel the tug of the cracker.

While the whip is traveling backward over your shoulder, push the whip forward under the backward path. Your hand should make a little circle in front of you, like the drive arm of a train.

The whip will form an S-shape as it catches up with itself. The loop will roll forward.

Aim and squeeze. You can tell the whip where to crack.

Follow through with the whip along the same line, swinging it behind you into the air so the cracker is now traveling forward from behind you over your head, your arm extended behind you. (FIG. 2)

You can encourage the whip to flow along a straight line by keeping the handle parallel to your body, forward and backward.

In the Reverse Circus Crack, swing whip upward behind you, extending your arm to keep whip on a straight line.

Keep elbow in to side. The forward part of the crack is like flipping a Frisbee underhand. The whip cracks as it rises, and this rising arc can be the start of a new Slow Figure 8.

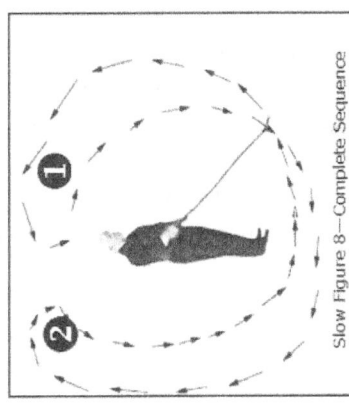

Slow Figure 8—Complete Sequence

## THE PERFECT WHIP THROW

I was researching material to expand my knowledge of cravat tying so I could make my Wild West costumes more era-authentic.

I came across a Cabinet Magazine article by Brian Dillon titled "A Poet of the Cloth," about Beau Brummel's approach to sartorial sophistication. Dillon's words could just as easily be applied to whip cracking. The parallels were beyond eerie – they were uncanny.

The article analyzed H. Le Blanc's 1828 book, "The Art of Tying the Cravat," illustrated with examples like the easy going "L'Americain" cravat, and the more sinuous and sensual "Sentimentale." In one paragraph, the author captured the essence of the art of cravat tying:

"What the wearer (of a cravat) is after is a 'curious mean' between skill and pure chance... the knot is intentional, but the folds are entirely fortuitous..."

This phrase reminded me of the contradictions which abound in the realms of pure whip cracking. The perfect throw is often an unintended side effect. A seemingly effortless whip handling is usually the result years of conscientious and determined practice.

I have engaged in a lifelong pursuit of the Marvelous, but even I was surprised to see the principles of Power and Transformation (my personal household gods) combine in cravat tying to change an ordinary instant into an event of alchemical beauty. This moment validates the Divine that flows through us rather than from us, the way the energy wave flow through the whip instead of from it.

I was grateful for this article, a postcard from the Universe reminding me one should never, ever settle for mere perfection.

## WHIPS AS EXERCISE

I once was asked, "Do you know how many calories you burn by practicing with a bullwhip or during a show?"

The question intrigued me. I used 20 minutes as my baseline for a 200-pound person. The best I could do was to compare various activities for the same amount of time, since energy expenditure levels can have a large variance over the same time.

**Gentle Workout Equivalent**
Stationary rowing, moderate  212 calories
Kayaking  151
Frisbee General  136
Golf: walking and pulling clubs  130
Ti Chi  121
Archery, non-hunting  106
Walking at 3mph (20 min/mile)  100

**Performance Equivalent**
Martial Arts – judo, karate, kick boxing, tae kwan do  303
Soccer general  212
Fencing  180

This info was gleaned from http://www.primusweb.com/cgibin/fpc/actcalc.pl

The length of the whip (and consequently, its weight) also makes a difference. And, of course, if you are working whips with both hands simultaneously, the results will be much higher.

## ONE DOZEN WAYS TO IMPROVE ACCURACY

Most people make the same mistakes when they are beginners. But they also tend to make the same mistakes as each other when they are well along in their whip-cracking experience. One of these off-the-shelf solutions might help you solve the problem of being more accurate with a six-foot bullwhip.

**1. Check your whip.** Look for tangles or knots in the fall or cracker. Make sure your whip is conditioned so it will roll smoothly. Pay special attention to the fall, because this will require more greasing than the thong will.

**2. Use a sword fighter stance.** This will align your whole body more with the throw and end the problems caused by your torquing your body (and the whip).

**3. Keep the whip's handle parallel to your body.** Keep your arm extended along a vertical line so you can aim straight down your forearm, hand and handle. Go a bit slower, but with enough "oomph" to keep the whip in the air.

**4. Remember that a hrow starts behind you.** With the Overhand Flick, hoist the whip up behind you higher than your shoulder so you are throwing downhill. Shooting downward automatically increases your accuracy.

**5. Use the Point and Squeeze technique.** Especially at the point of the pop. Use the Overhand Flick for a precise throw at a point in space. Use the Circus Crack for cutting down a straight line, and where depth is not a factor.

**6. Remember that different cracks have different depths.** With the Overhand Flick, the whip cracks at the end of the fully extended fall and popper. With the Circus Crack, the whip cracks 2/3 to ¾ down the length of the whip away from you. The depths are different for these two cracks, but they are consistent in themselves.

**7. Use the belly of the whip .** The whip wants to roll along the belly-spine axis. If your throw is off the line of the belly, or if your hand torques the whip off the line of the belly, it will flip and flop at the end of the crack.

**8. Try going a bit slower.** A muscled whip is not as accurate as a rlaxed one. You will still get the power you want by exaggerating the movement as you go a little slower. Remember: Go Big, Go Slow.

**9. Use a shorter whip.** You'll be standing closer to your target.

**10. Pay attention to the wind.** It might not seem like much to you, but that little popper can become a kite in a gale at the end of your fall.

**11. Compensate.** Pick a target and throw the whip. See how far you miss, and in what direction. Compensate exactly this amount for your following throws. Usually, you need to do this only a few times at the beginning of a performance or show. Sometimes it's your form, but sometimes it's the whip itself. It may be retaining its memory of how it was coiled and stored. Just as you need to warm up, your whip does, as well.

**12. Relax your ass.** No kidding! It's a very effective dancer's trick, because when you let go of the stress and tension in your buttocks, your whole body relaxes. And all that communicates into the whip.

www.ingramcontent.com/pod-product-compliance
Lightning Source LLC
LaVergne TN
LVHW081450060526
838201LV00050BA/1761